Reptiles and Amphibians
of
Red River Gorge
and the
Greater Red River Basin
Second Edition

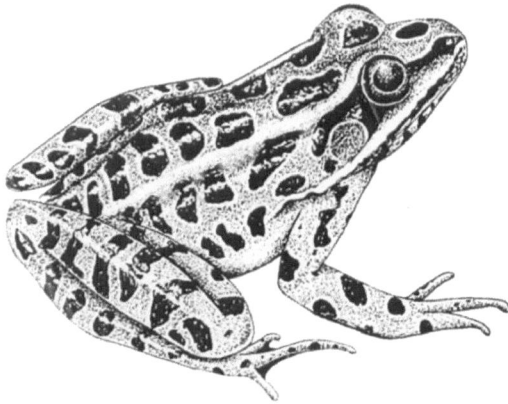

Written by
Dan & Judy Dourson

Photos and Illustrations by Dan Dourson
unless otherwise stated

2021

Published by
Goatslug Publications
1128 Gritter Ridge Road, Stanton, Kentucky, USA

Goatslug Publications

Front cover: Eastern Hog-nosed Snake

This book is designed to present general information and anecdotal accounts about reptiles and amphibians of the Red River Gorge and Greater Red River Basin. Limitations of space prevent the inclusion of in-depth details about the herpetofauna of the area. For further information about the herpetofauna, refer to the bibliography in the back of the book.

Nomenclature for this book follows Society for the Study of Amphibians and Reptiles (SSAR). https://ssarherps.org/

Contents

Impetus For The Book

The original list of reptiles and amphibians of the Red River Gorge was developed in the early 1970's by John MacGregor through a combination of extensive field work, examination and verification of specimens held in numerous museum and university collections, and review of herpetological literature. This information was then incorporated into the USFS Stanton Ranger District 1989 Inventory and a checklist was developed for the first Herpetology Weekend in 1991. Since then, the Annual Herpetology Weekend has provided additional records for the reptiles and amphibians of the Red River Gorge.

This book compiles the above information into one pictorial guide and should be useful to participants of Herpetology Weekend, visitors to the Red River Gorge, landowners, natural resource managers, medical personnel, and residents of eastern Kentucky.

Acknowledgments

We would like to thank the following agencies, organizations, and individuals for their contributions to this publication. We couldn't have done it without you!

Mark Gumbert Copperhead Consulting, for financial support to publish the first edition of the book, use of images, field trip leader, and guest speaker for Herpetology Weekends; *James Kiser* Stantec, field trip leader and frequent speaker at Herpetology Weekends; *Price Sewell* and *Rob Stinson* Copperhead Consulting, for searching and scanning images used throughout the text; *Brian Gasdorf, & Andrew Stevens,* Natural Bridge State Park Naturalists, for permission to photograph turtles from the park; *Kentucky Reptile Zoo* for the opportunity to photograph several zoo animals; *Les and Michelle Meade,* for their generous contribution to help publish the first edition and field trip leaders for Herpetology Weekends; *Howard Branham*, who found the first record of juvenile Red Cornsnake in the Red River Gorge; *Aaron Dourson, amy batchman dourson, Finn Oliver Dourson, Jonathan, Jill, Elijah, Reuben, Kalilah, & Pearl Hicks* for finding Herps to photograph for the book; *Colby and Angela Christensen* for donating the use of their rental cabin at The Wilds (Mesodon Farm) for Herpetology Weekend trip leaders and speakers; *Morgan Hockensmith* (a camper) for rescuing my turtle traps from the Red River that were nearly swept away in an overnight flood; *Jayd Raines* and *Torrey Stegall* for help locating several species (i.e. Midland Mud) to photograph; and Dr. Stephen Richter and his copperhead research team, *Jocelyn Hendricks, Jesse Sockman,* and *Henderson Gull* for the excellent article.

Thanks to the following persons for use of their great images: *John MacGregor, Will Bird, Phil Peak, Kory G. Roberts, Steve Bonney, Les Meade, Jr., Mark Gumbert,* and finally, *Sarah Phillips* for her amazing images of copperheads eating cicadas

A sincere thanks to *John MacGregor* for his thorough and critical review of the text. John's comments improved the book immensely. Furthermore, much of the natural history information under "Species Accounts" comes from John's extensive knowledge of Kentucky's herpetofauna.

Maps: Red River Watershed map from *Christopher McNees*, Copperhead Consulting, web images, and others from Google Maps.

.

Valued Supporters of Herpetology Weekend

Kentucky Dept. of Fish & Wildlife Resources

KENTUCKY STATE PARKS
"the nation's finest"

COPPERHEAD
ENVIRONMENTAL CONSULTING

KENTUCKY
REPTILE ZOO

theZOO
LOUISVILLE

Red River Gorge*ous*
Wilderness Cabin Rentals

Stantec

Greater Cincinnati Herpetological Society

FOREST SERVICE
U S
DEPARTMENT OF AGRICULTURE

Kentucky Herpetological Society

Hoosier Herpetological Society

Adult Red Cornsnake, Red River Gorge, Powell County Kentucky

Juvenile Red Cornsnake, Red River Gorge, Powell County Kentucky

John MacGregor

Introduction

One of nature's finest examples of creative erosion lies within Kentucky's Cumberland Plateau region. This visually stunning natural area known as Red River Gorge (RRG) is a place of extreme geophysical expressions and surprising biodiversity. Through eons of time, the Red River has carved a 600-foot-deep gorge through 300-million-year-old sandstone. Rising above a sea of jade-colored forests are more than 900 miles of soaring cliff-lines, 700+ sandstone arches, and numerous cascading waterfalls. But the Red River Gorge is only a small portion of a bigger basin. As the river continues on its meander, it slices through the prominent **Knobs** section of the state, and a small portion of the **Outer Bluegrass** before emptying into the Kentucky River.

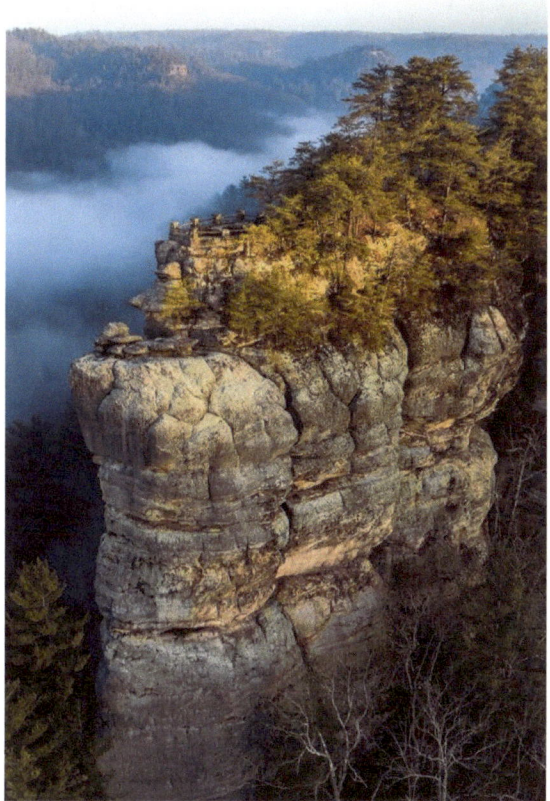

Chimney Top Rock, Red River Gorge, Web image

Without question, the Red River Gorge is the "crowning jewel" of the watershed, harboring a remarkable variety of uncommon ecological zones and microclimates. These diverse biomes have anchored a tremendous number of plant and animal species, and one might argue, the most interesting herpetofauna of the basin. The single biggest contributing factor to the Gorge's wealth of species is undeniably the massive sandstone cliffs. These towering rock formations have shaped a myriad of divergent ecosystems from pine-covered ridgetops to cool humid gorges.

Red River Gorge has been designated a National Geological Area, National Natural Landmark, National Archaeological District, and is on the National Register of Historic Places. The Gorge includes an area of around 30,000 acres or 45 square miles. Clifty Wilderness, at approximately 14,000 acres (20 square miles), is the largest of two designated wilderness areas in Kentucky. In 1993, a 20-mile portion of the nearly 100-mile-long Red River was listed as a National Wild and Scenic River for its exceptional quality and unparalleled aesthetic values.

While most of the 66 species of reptiles and amphibians in the Red River Watershed are found throughout the basin, there are a number of species partitioned by the three geophysical regions described above. For example, Queensnakes are common in streams in the Outer Bluegrass but absent from the Knobs and Cumberland Plateau. Upland Chorus Frogs and Northern Zigzag Salamanders are also missing from these regions, occurring only in or near lower portions of the watershed. Blanchard's Cricket Frogs are found in the Knobs and Outer Bluegrass but not the Cumberland Plateau. Green Salamanders occur almost exclusively in sandstone cliffs, a geological feature missing from the Outer Bluegrass. Allegheny Mountain Dusky and Black Mountain Salamanders are restricted to the Cumberland Plateau. Other reptiles and amphibians are less clear in terms of distribution. The elusive Scarletsnake is so rarely observed that it is nearly impossible to ascertain populations and distribution within the watershed.

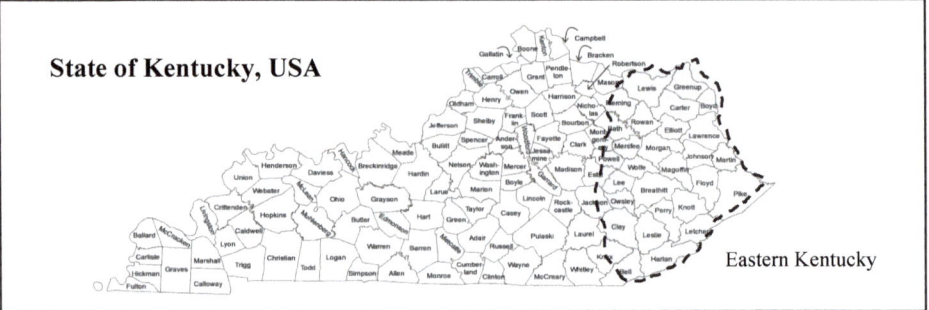

State of Kentucky, USA

Eastern Kentucky

The area covered by this book includes the entire Red River Basin, a small portion of the Outer Bluegrass and most of Eastern Kentucky (in shaded and dashed lines above and below).

Eastern Kentucky

Red River Basin

5

The Red River Basin, Eastern Kentucky, USA

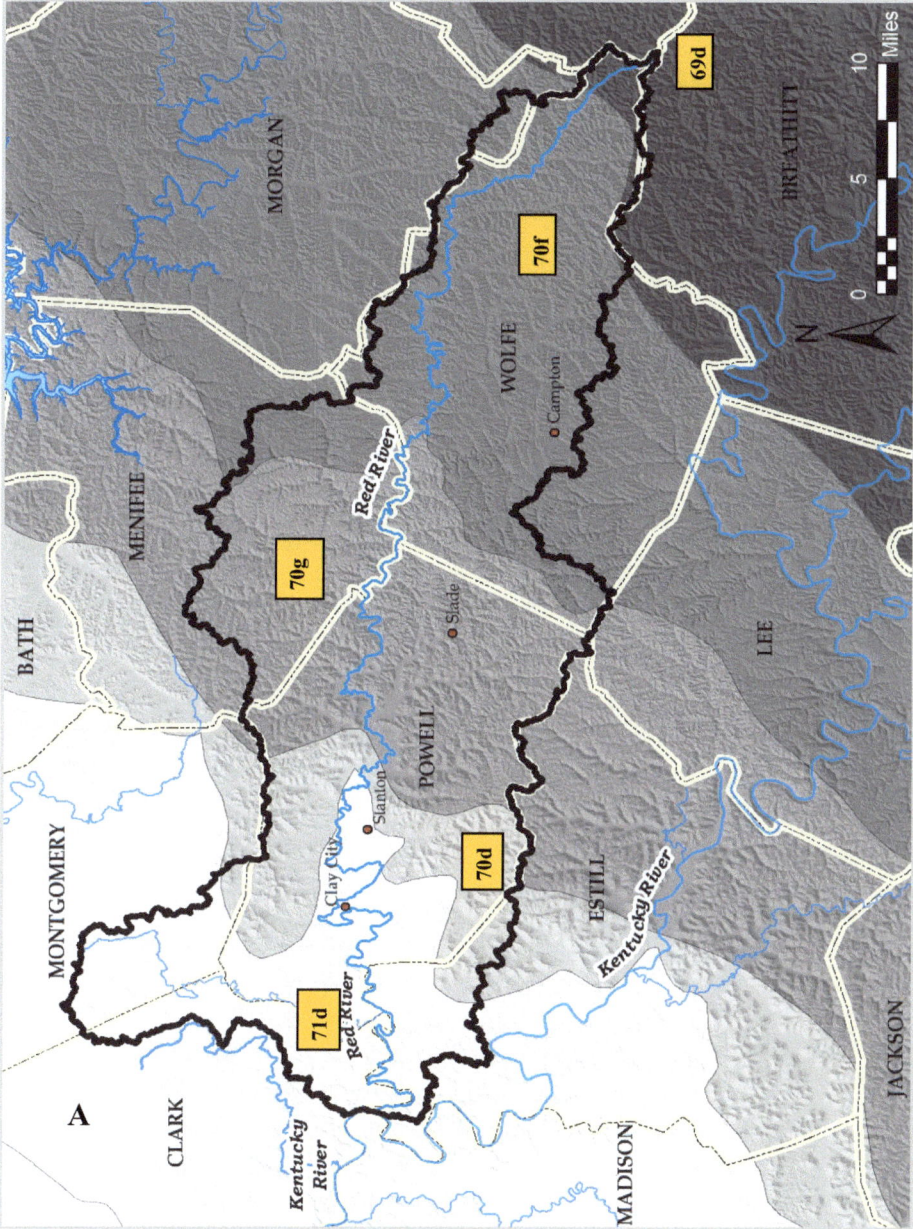

Level IV Ecoregions of the Red River Watershed (Woods *et al.* 1998), including County Lines and Towns (map © Christopher McNees, *Copperhead Consulting*)

71d. Outer Bluegrass
70d. Knobs–Lower Scioto Dissected Plateau
70g. Northern Forested Plateau Escarpment
70f. Ohio/Kentucky Carboniferous Plateau
69d. Dissected Appalachian Plateau

Herpetofauna of Red River Gorge and Greater Red River Basin

AMPHIBIANS (36 confirmed species)
Salamanders are well-known and highly valued members of temperate forests and are found from deep limestone caves to dry ridgetops. There are 22 confirmed species of salamanders known to occur within the Red River Basin, and one species, the Northern Zigzag Salamander, within a few miles of the watershed (see map opposite page). Although Tiger and Mole Salamanders were introduced to the area, recent 2017 surveys suggest that they did not survive. While most salamanders are relatively common, four species including Black Mountain, Allegheny Mountain Dusky, Cumberland Plateau, and Hellbender are all considered uncommon residents of the basin.

Frogs and Toads (Anurans) are represented by 14 species, with one species, the Eastern Narrow-mouthed Toad introduced to the watershed (see map opposite page). There are records of Upland Chorus Frogs from the nearby town of Irvine (see map opposite page). From quarter-sized Blanchard's CricketFrogs to copious American Bullfrogs the size of dinner plates, anurans can be found from valley floors to sandstone ridgetops. More often heard than seen, frogs and toads rule the night sounds with their varied calls, backed by copious numbers. One need only stand in the middle of several hundred calling Spring Peepers to be humbled by the ear-piercing songs.

REPTILES (25 confirmed species)
Snakes comprise 18 confirmed species in the Red River Basin and one species, the Scarlet Kingsnake, close to the watershed (see map opposite page). Snakes are by far the most commonly encountered and memorable reptiles in RRG. The longest snake is the Gray Ratsnake at around 6 feet. In terms of absolute body mass, however, the Timber Rattlesnake has the honor of being the largest. Species like the Common Wormsnake exhibit little color-contrast while the Scarletsnake is a spectacular example of color-evolution. Of the 18 species of snakes, only two are venomous, the Rattlesnake and the Copperhead. Considerable color variation exists within snake species found in the Red River Basin.

Lizards are represented by 5 species in the Red River Basin. The tiny Little Brown Skink is by far the most common species, usually seen only briefly, escaping under debris when threatened. In contrast, the Broad-headed Skink can grow over a foot long and is highly arboreal in trees. Like snakes and turtles, all lizards are ectothermic, meaning core body temperature remains close to or at the temperature of their surroundings. This explains why lizards are often seen basking in the sun—a behavior not shared by salamanders who prefer hiding under moist leaf-litter, logs, and rocks.

Turtles are represented by 8 species that reside in or near the Red River Basin, with 7 species decisively aquatic and one species—the Eastern Box Turtle—entirely terrestrial. Of the eight turtle species, the Eastern Box Turtle is the only one capable of completely closing up its shell—a defense against predators—while the other 7 species rely on aquatic systems to hide from potential danger. Although relatively common, aquatic turtles are the least observed reptiles in Red River Gorge.

Additional Species of Interest

Species Close To The Red River Basin But Not Yet Documented

▢ Upland Chorus Frog, *Pseudacris feriarum*
▢ Scarlet Kingsnake, *Lampropeltis elapsoides*
▢ Northern Zigzag Salamander, *Plethodon dorsalis*

Species Introduced to Cane Creek Watershed and Gritter Ridge, Powell County

▢ Eastern Narrow-mouthed Toad, *Gastrophryne carolinensis*

Tiger Salamanders were introduced on Gritter Ridge in 1993 (GPS 37°46'12.3"N, 83°45'08.6"W). Tiger and Mole Salamanders were also introduced into the Cane Creek Watershed in 1996 (GPS 37°52'51"N, 83°45'24"W). During the months of February and early March of 2017, extensive trapping (two drift fences, 8 minnow traps in 4 ponds) along with night-surveys of same ponds at the Cane Creek site were conducted by the authors. No Tiger or Mole Salamanders were caught or observed at this time. It is therefore assumed that the introduction of these two species at that location was unsuccessful. The Gritter Ridge site has not had a follow-up investigation, however in March of 1997, Greg Lipps found a gravid Tiger Salamander crossing HY 1639 near Sand Lick (GPS 37°46.945N, 83°43.912W) in a flood plain area of the South Fork of the Red River. This location is around 1.4 miles from the ridgetop release site on Gritter Ridge.

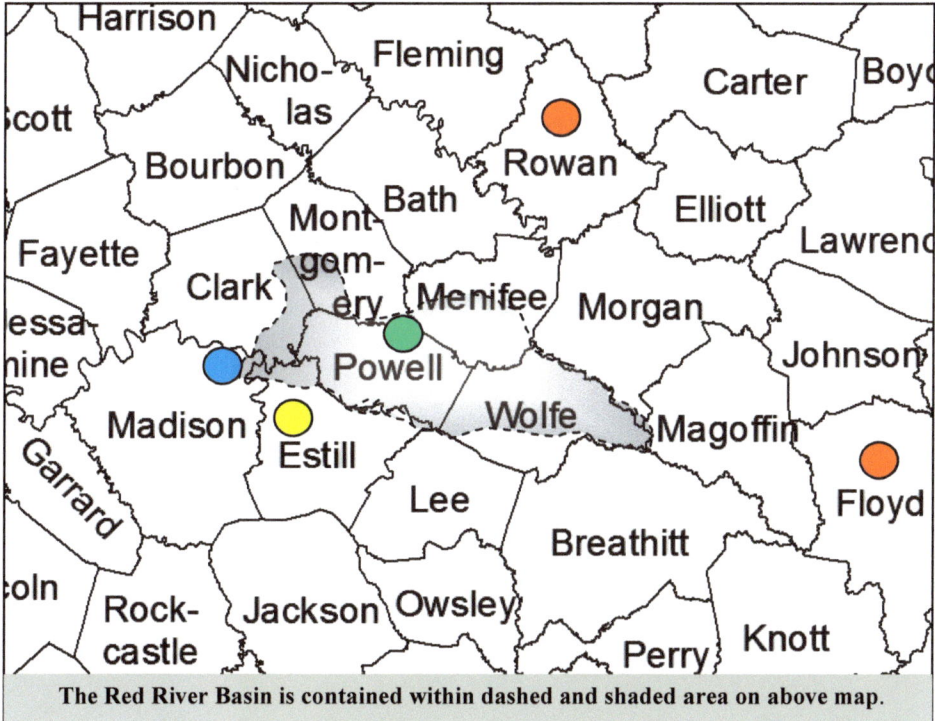

The Red River Basin is contained within dashed and shaded area on above map.

8

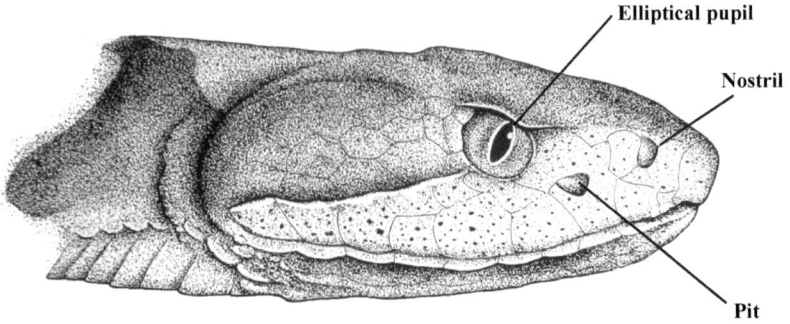

In Kentucky, *venomous* snakes have **elliptical pupils** and heat sensing pits (Copperhead).

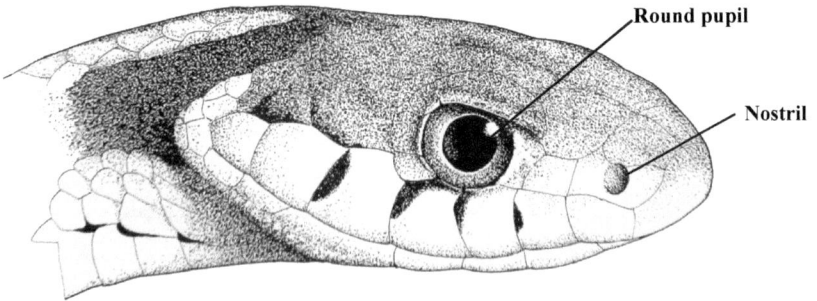

In Kentucky, *non-venomous* snakes have **round pupils** and no pits (Gartersnake).

Underside of snake tail, below anal plate

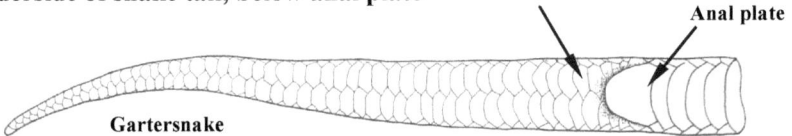

In Kentucky, all *non-venomous* snakes have a double row of scales beyond the anal plate.

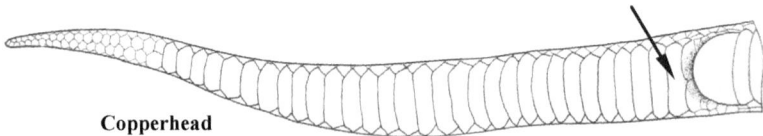

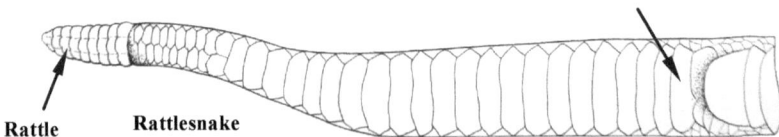

In Kentucky, all *venomous* snakes have a single row of scales beyond the anal plate.

9

Basic Reptile and Amphibian Morphology—Lizards

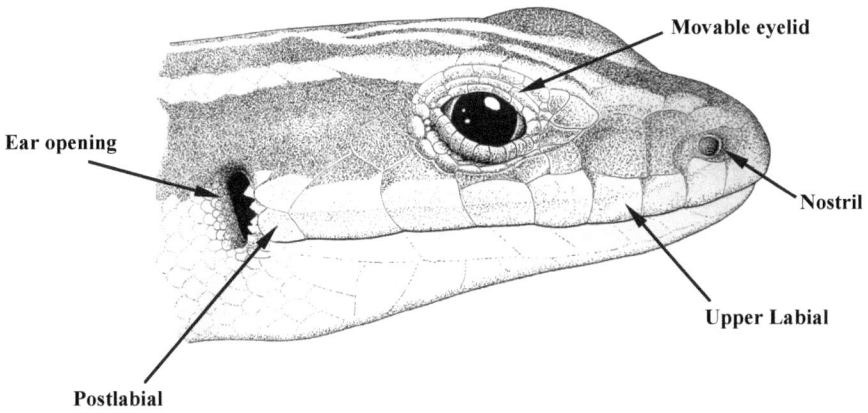

Common Five-lined Skink

Basic Reptile and Amphibian Morphology—Turtles

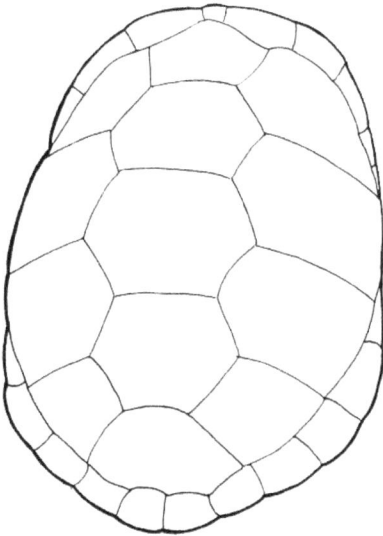

Carapace (top of shell)   Plastron (bottom of shell)

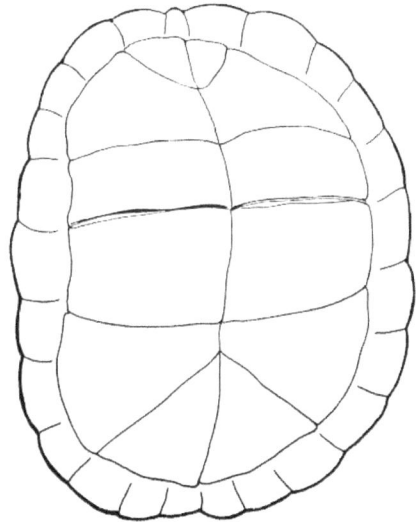

The Basic Salamander

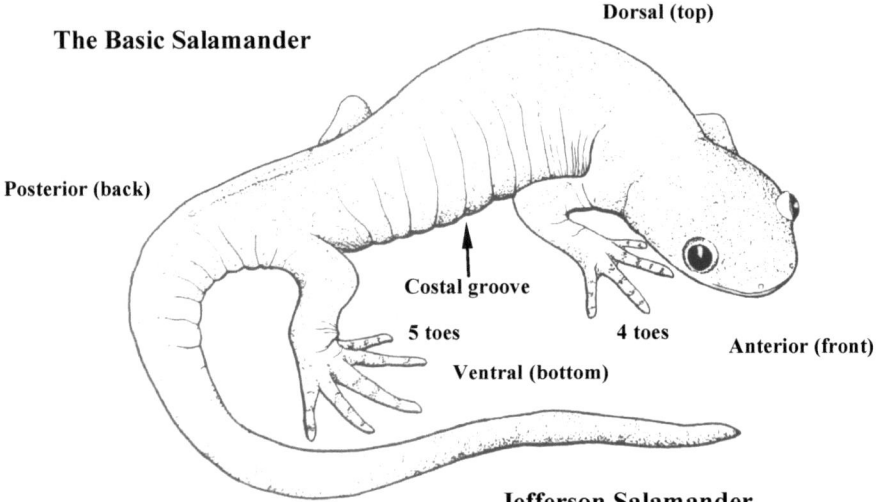

Dorsal (top)

Posterior (back)

Costal groove

5 toes

4 toes

Ventral (bottom)

Anterior (front)

Jefferson Salamander

Ventral side of salamander

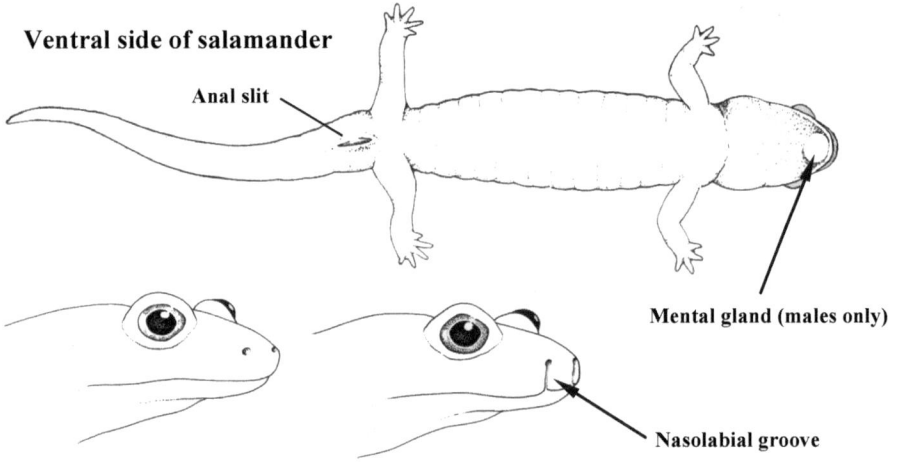

Anal slit

Mental gland (males only)

Nasolabial groove

Amplexing Eastern Newts

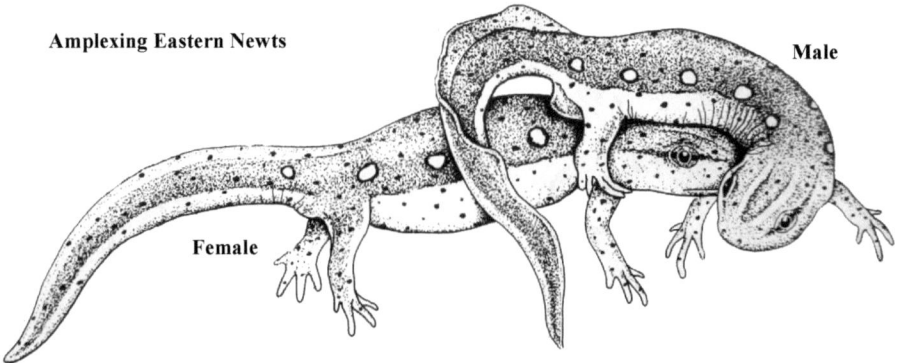

Male

Female

Mental Glands of Plethodontid Salamanders

Southern Ravine Salamander,
Plethodon richmondi

Northern Zigzag Salamander,
Plethodon dorsalis

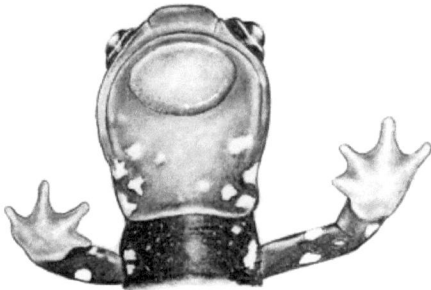

Cumberland Plateau Salamander,
Plethodon kentucki

Northern Slimy Salamander,
Plethodon glutinosus

Mental gland

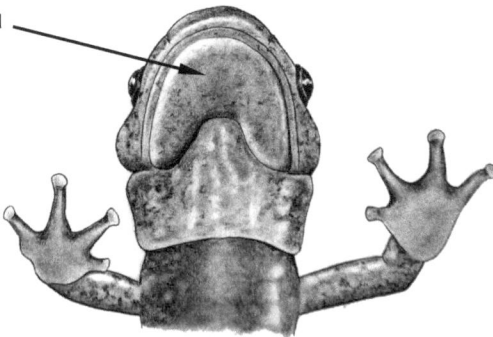

Green Salamander, *Aneides aeneus*

In Plethodontid salamanders, the **mental gland** of the male secretes pheromones that are delivered to the female by slapping or stabbing the mental gland across the female's vomeronasal organ (VNO) located on her snout (Arnold 1976). Mental gland shapes can also be used to distinguish various species in the Plethodontidae family (see above).

The Basic Frog

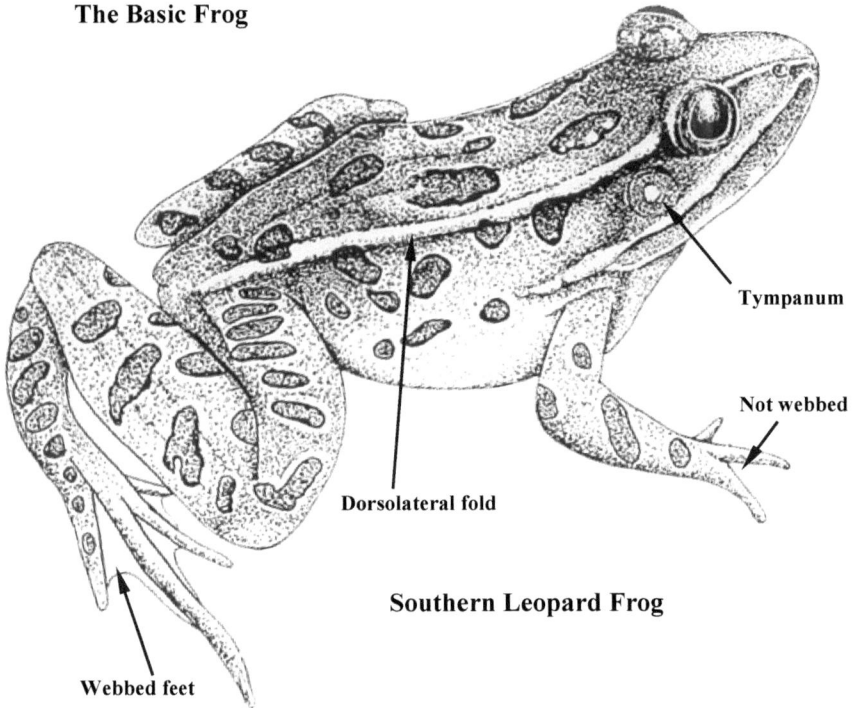

Tympanum

Not webbed

Dorsolateral fold

Southern Leopard Frog

Webbed feet

The Basic Tadpole

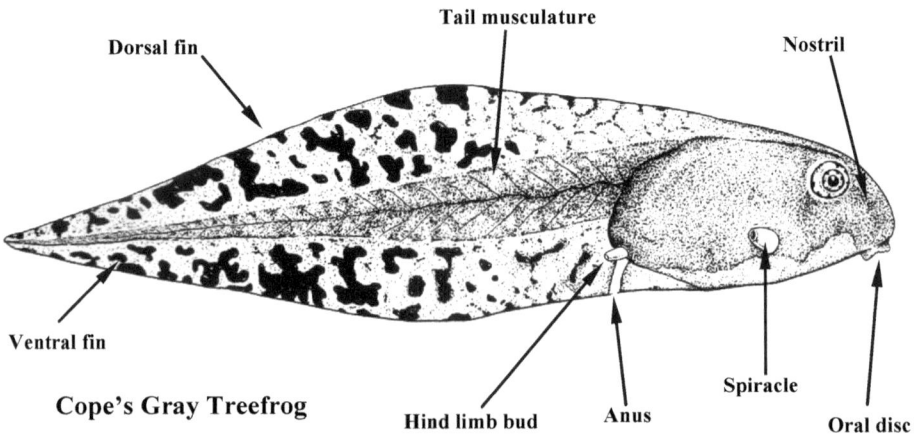

Tail musculature

Nostril

Dorsal fin

Ventral fin

Cope's Gray Treefrog

Hind limb bud

Anus

Spiracle

Oral disc

13

Tympanum

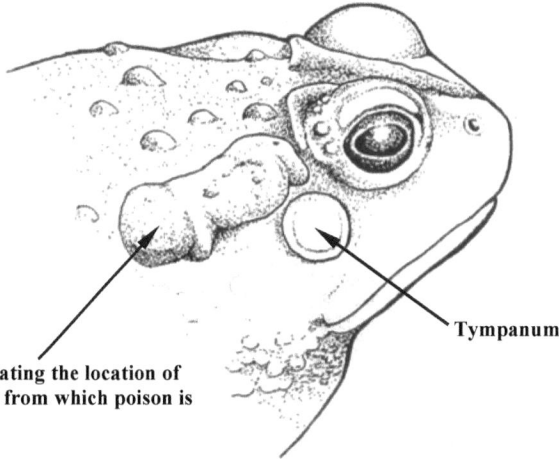

A toad head illustrating the location of
the Parotoid gland from which poison is
discharged

Digging spur

Hind foot of Spadefoot Toad   Hind foot of American Toad

Species Accounts

Each illustrated species contains common name, scientific name, and general size of the animal (example: **Spotted Salamander,** *Ambystoma maculatum.* 5-9 in.). This is followed by general habitat, description, and comparisons to similar species. Lastly, in parenthesis is a regional code (see below), time of year most commonly encountered, frequency, and where the animal was photographed (example: CP,KN,OB, spring, common, Cane Creek, Powell Co, KY). Animal locations photographed by other biologists are generally with those individual names (example: John MacGregor, Powell Co, KY) on the right lower side of the photograph.

<u>**Regional Codes used under "Species Accounts"**</u>
CP-Cumberland Plateau
KN-Knobs
OB-Outer Bluegrass
RRG-Red River Gorge

Eastern copperheads, RRG, Powell Co, Kentucky

Species Accounts

A gravid Spotted Salamander, RRG, Powell County, Kentucky

The eye-catching Marbled Salamander, RRG, Powell County, Kentucky

Salamanders

Occasionally mistaken for lizards, salamanders are amphibians that have smooth, moist skin while lizards are reptiles with dry, scaly skin and sharp claws at the ends of each toe. In Red River Gorge, lizards are generally found in drier habitats and are often observed basking in the sun while salamanders hide in the shadows of moist places during the heat of the day.

Salamanders, along with other smaller organisms, are often regarded as inconsequential players in healthy functioning ecosystems but nothing could be further from the truth. Believe it or not, in some environments like the Great Smoky Mountains National Park, the biomass of salamanders alone can outweigh all other vertebrate animals (mammals, birds reptiles, and fish) combined. With such vast numbers crawling through the leaf litter, they no doubt have tremendous value in terrestrial ecosystems.

Salamanders, unique among vertebrates, can regenerate lost arms, feet, toes, and other damaged body parts. Brightly-colored species like the Spotted and Marbled Salamanders defend themselves by producing a milky substance in the skin when under attack. These chemical compounds are distasteful to predators.

While several species of salamanders have typical lungs for breathing, salamanders in the family Plethodontidae (mostly woodland species) are without lungs and breathe through their skin which is accomplished by a network of superficial blood vessels near the skin's surface and to a lesser degree tissues lining the mouth.

Most salamanders are active at night during the spring rainy season and late fall. During the day, salamanders usually remain well-concealed under logs and rocks or in the case of the mole salamanders—Spotted, Streamside, Marbled, and Jefferson— in deep burrows. As summer heats up, most salamanders go deeper to escape the drier and warmer temperatures and thus, are harder to locate during this time of year. The few exceptions are Black Mountain, Seal, Northern Dusky, and Southern Two-lined Salamanders—which remain active in or near streams, so are not subject to the heat and moisture stresses of other salamanders. Green Salamanders can usually be found in narrow crevices of sandstone clifflines without much difficulty.

Salamanders lay eggs in a variety of locations. While Mole Salamanders (*Ambystoma*) lay eggs in vernal ponds, woodland salamanders (*Plethodon*) hide their eggs in caves, deep under rock talus, underground, or in the case of the Green Salamander, in sandstone crevices. The beautiful Spotted Salamander, *Ambystoma maculatum,* attaches its eggs to submerged sticks in small woodland ponds (below a female Spotted Salamander laying eggs, Powell County, Kentucky).

A female Spotted Salamander laying eggs on a stick in small woodland pond, RRG

Although most salamanders are relatively small, there are giants living among sunken boulders in the Red River. One such species is the Eastern Hellbender, *Cryptobrancchus alleganiensis.* Nearly two feet in length, this ogre among salamanders (opposite page) is rarely seen, moving stealthily along the bottom of the river at night, searching for its primary cuisine of soft-shelled crayfish. Eastern Hellbenders are occasionally caught by uninformed fisherman who often kill these harmless salamanders.

19

Eastern Hellbender,
The Ogre of Salamanders

Mark Gumbert, Licking River , KY

One of the most common salamanders of the basin includes the Eastern Newt. Found in nearly every body of water, Eastern Newts are chemically protected in ponds containing predatory fish and are highly predacious on the eggs of frogs and salamanders. The Red Eft (terrestrial stage of the Eastern Newt) sports bright orange and red colors that warn of the salamander's skin which contains the powerful poison **tetrodotoxin** (a potent neurotoxin). Having little fear of being eaten, the Red Eft is often seen parading around the forest floor after summer rains and few predators will risk a meal of this potentially fatal amphibian.

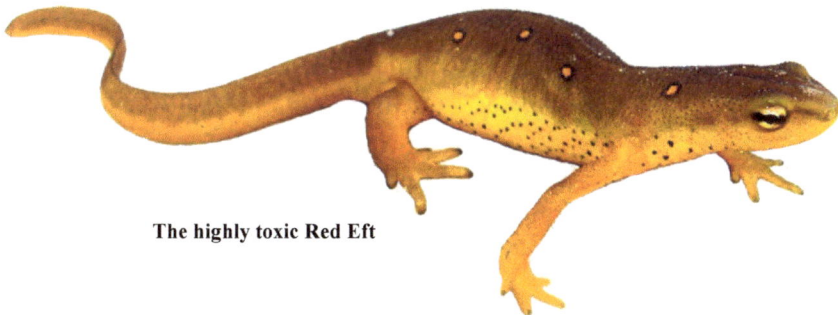

The highly toxic Red Eft

Red River Gorge has a rich salamander diversity with at least 22 confirmed species. The following pages illustrate the remarkable variety, size, and color patterns of these remarkable creatures. Although secretive animals by nature, if one looks in the right places at the right time of year, these slippery jewels can be found without much effort.

Marbled Salamander

Marbled Salamander, *Ambystoma opacum.* (3-4 inches). This handsome mole salamander lives in wooded regions throughout the Basin. Although a common species, Marbled Salamanders are rarely observed outside the breeding season since they are fossorial,
living deep within underground burrows. The only time they can be readily found is during heavy fall rains either crossing roads after dark to breeding ponds or at the ponds. To
find these salamanders, carefully look under logs at pond edges for females sitting on
clutches of eggs. After ponds fill from rain, females abandon the eggs and return to burrows not to be seen for another year. Nature's perfect biological mosquito control are
newly hatching salamander larvae (opposite page, bottom image), which consume vast
numbers of mosquito larvae and other small invertebrates. By early summer, the larvae
are transforming (metamorphosis) into a terrestrial form (sub-adult), at which time, they
move to life on land for as much as 30 years. Other mole salamanders including the Spotted and Jefferson Salamanders are also pond breeders and have similar life stages.
(CP,KN,OB, fall, common, Martins Fork, RRG, Powell Co, KY).

Unusual pattern

Marbled Salamander

Female with eggs

Eight-week old Marbled Salamander larvae with their feather-like gills used to absorb oxygen

Metamorphosing Marbled Salamander

Spotted Salamander

Spotted Salamander, *Ambystoma maculatum.* (5-9 inc.). Spotted Salamanders are one of the most colorful, wide-ranging, and common salamanders in eastern North America. The species typically has a double row of yellow spots positioned on a dark dorsal with lighter ventral sides. Occasionally head spots are orange (page 26). The mating ritual of the Spotted Salamander is a performance worthy of closer observation. On the first or second continuous night of rain in late winter when temperatures reach 45-50 degrees F, male and female Spotted Salamanders migrate from woodland burrows, often crossing roads to fish-free ponds by the hundreds. This marvelous ritual is often referred to as the "Big Night" by herpetologists. But the real show begins at the pond. Over-anxious males are the first to arrive, forming large breeding balls called congresses. As the females arrive, a male separates from the congress and performs a courtship dance with a female. The pair will circle each other, putting their heads under each others' tails. The male may climb on the female's back or rub her with his chin. If she is agreeable, he then leads her to a spot in the bottom of the pond where he has previously deposited his spermatophore packets. She uses her cloaca to pick up the packet and the eggs are fertilized internally. She may collect packets from several males. Egg masses the size of golf balls are laid on submerged vegetation attached to sticks in the pond (opposite page, top image). As they fill with water, they expand to the size of softballs and are firm to the touch. The larvae hatch in about 6 weeks and by mid-summer metamorphose and climb out of the pond where they begin a life on land. Believe it or not, Spotted Salamanders can be lured from the depths of the pond by simply placing your hand in the water at the pond's edge and wiggling your fingers. Males will come right up to your hand, even nudging your finger tips, thinking it's a female who has just arrived at the pond. (CP,KN,OB, fall, common, Martins Fork, RRG, Powell Co, KY).

Spotted Salamander

Female Spotted Salamander laying eggs in pond

Spotted Salamander larvae

Metamorphosing Spotted Salamander

Mark Gumbert

24

Spotted Salamander

A Spotted Salamander with unusually large spots, Cane Creek, Powell Co, KY

A Spotted Salamander with unusually small, faded spots, Cane Creek, Powell Co, KY

Spotted Salamander

Spotted Salamanders will occasionally have orange spots on head, Spencer Co, KY

Three Spotted Salamanders from the same breeding pond, Cane Creek, Powell Co, KY.

Jefferson Salamander

Jefferson Salamander, *Ambystoma jeffersonianum.* (5-8 inches). The Jefferson Salamander has a long flattened snout, blade-like tail, excessively long toes, and is dark (with or without bluish flecks). Breeding anytime from late fall to early spring, it is not uncommon to see these cold-tolerant amphibians under a sheet of ice in small, woodland ponds. Egg masses are the size of golf balls and less firm than Spotted Salamander eggs. (CP,KN,OB, spring, common, all specimens from RRG area, Powell Co, KY).

Jefferson Salamander

Above left image of a Jefferson Salamander just caught from a pond and above right photo of same animal out of water 8 hours later. Note the interesting color difference, an adaptation that likely serves as a protective, habitat matching strategy.

Jefferson Salamander eggs

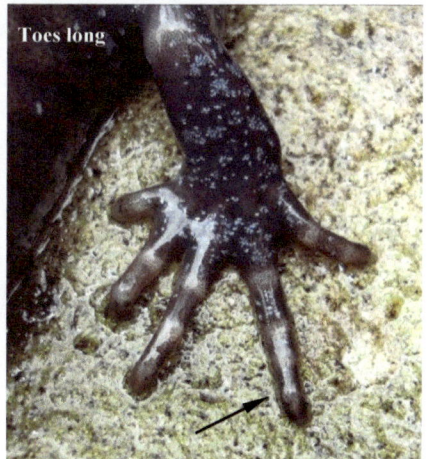

Toes long

Streamside Salamander

Thick tail

Streamside Salamander, _Ambystoma barbouri._ (4-6 inches). A Streamside Salamander is similar to a Jefferson Salamander but has a chunkier build with a blunt head. Jefferson Salamanders are anorexic-looking and their heads are longer and more shovel-shaped (page 27). Streamside Salamander also has shorter toes than the Jefferson Salamander (page 28). Tail of the Streamside Salamander is extremely thick. A species of floodplains, usually breeding mid-winter to early spring. Eggs laid in ditches, swampy woodlands, and ponds are attached singly to roots, fallen limbs, dead leaves, vegetation, and other debris as well as on the undersides of rocks (opposite page). (CP,KN,OB, spring, common, all Streamside Salamander photos except eggs from Cane Creek, Powell Co, KY).

Head roundish and thick

Streamside Salamander

Toes of Streamside Salamander are notably shorter than Jefferson Salamander (pg. 28 for comparison)

Female with eggs in stream under rock

John MacGregor, Jessamine Co, KY

Spring Salamander

Spring Salamander, *Gyrinophilus porphyriticus*. (5-8 inches). A robust species of seeps and springs, Spring Salamanders are similar to Red and Midland Mud Salamanders but have a notably longer snout. Like many salamanders, it can be found crossing roads during rainy nights. Diet includes a variety of invertebrates and other salamanders. Eggs are laid underwater attached to rocks in seeps. Larvae live in slow moving streams and caves. Never put a Spring Salamander in with another salamander. It will be promptly devoured! (CP,KN,OB, common, RRG, Powell Co, KY).

Snout long, spots small and faded

Spring Salamander

Note the tiny, light spots on back

Young adults are lighter in color

Midland Mud Salamander

A lost tail in process of caudal-regeneration

Red lips

Midland Mud Salamander, *Pseudotriton montanus diastictus.* (3-6 inches). Similar to Red Salamander but with less crowded black spots. The Midland Mud Salamander has dark eyes and red lips while the Red Salamander has a line through its eyes and black lips. Adults inhabit moist or muddy sites around springs, swamps, bogs, and headwater tributaries of bottomlands but also dry ridgetops under logs in wet depressions. Diet depends largely on habitat and available food. Eggs deposited in same area and larva live there until maturation to a terrestrial form. (CP,KN,OB, spring, infrequent, bottomlands around Stanton next to Red River, Powell County, Kentucky).

Midland Mud Salamander

Juvenile from Bath County, KY

Red Salamander

A young adult Red Salamander

Red Salamander, *Pseudotriton ruber.* (4-6 inches). Although rarely seen, Red Salamanders are actually common throughout the Gorge. This species can be found under logs, large rocks, and wet leaf litter or crossing roads during rainy nights. Young individuals are brightly-colored becoming darker with age. Lips black (a). Diet consists of a variety of invertebrates. Eggs are laid underwater attached to rocks in seeps. Larvae live in slow-moving sections of streams. (CP,KN,OB, spring, common, all from RRG, Powell Co, KY).

Red Salamander

An aging adult Red Salamander

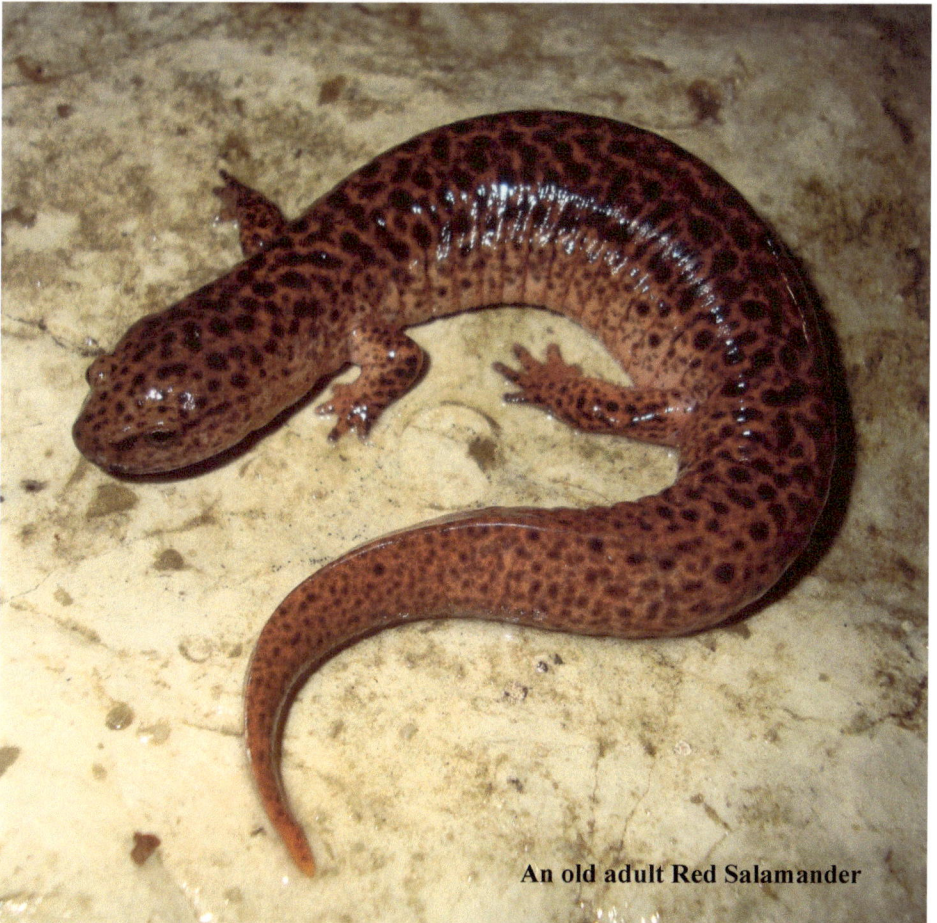

An old adult Red Salamander

Eastern Newt/Red Eft

A female Eastern Newt (note the wide, flat tail and smooth, slimy skin)

Eastern Newt/Red Eft, *Notophthalmus viridescens.* (2-4 inches). Eye of newt used in witches brew to turn a prince into a frog may be myths of fairytale stories but newts are the real Doctor Jekyll/Mr. Hyde of salamanders. This species lives a double life. The **Eastern Newt** (above image) is a slimy, aquatic form living in ponds and the **Red Eft** (bottom image) is a dry, warty salamander living on land. While both stages are chemically protected, the Red Eft is far more lethal. An Eastern Newt killed a young Snapping Turtle after ingestion (pers. comm. John MacGregor, 2016). The bright orange color of the Red Eft is a warning that it contains a powerful neurotoxin known as tetrodotoxin. The few predators that survive a meal of the Red Eft will steer clear of this noxious little amphibian next time around. Eastern Newts are common salamanders of nearly every kind of permanent or temporary wetland. (CP,KN,OB, common, Martins Fork, RRG, Powell Co, KY).

A male Red Eft (note the thin tail and dry, warty skin)

Eastern Newt/Red Eft

Bony crest of Red Eft

Amplexing newts in pond

Four-toed Salamander

Four-toed Salamander, *Hemidactylium scutatum.* (2-3 inches). A beautiful little salamander of rich woods. During the early spring breeding season, females migrate to small fishless ponds where eggs the size of BB's are deposited in clusters under moss-covered logs, rocks, and steep banks (pictured above a female on nest). There they remain with the eggs until hatching, at which time larvae drop directly into the pond. (CP,KN,OB, common, Martin's Fork, RRG, Powell Co, KY).

Four-toed Salamander

Constriction in tail will break off easily

4 toes on hind foot, other salamanders have 5

Belly white with black spots

40

Green Salamander

Green Salamander, *Aneides aeneus.* (3-5 inches). Built for the climb, the Green Salamander has expanded toe pads (a) for added friction, a flattened head to squeeze into tight places, and a prehensile tail (b) used as a fifth arm. Climbers beware! This little jewel can complete a 5.15c climb with its eyes closed! A charming salamander of moist, not wet, narrow sandstone crevices where eggs are attached to the ceiling and guarded by females (page 43, bottom image). Green Salamanders are also superbly colored and patterned to blend with lichens of the sandstone rock face. (CP,KN, common only in the Red River Gorge, Martins Fork, RRG, Powell Co, KY).

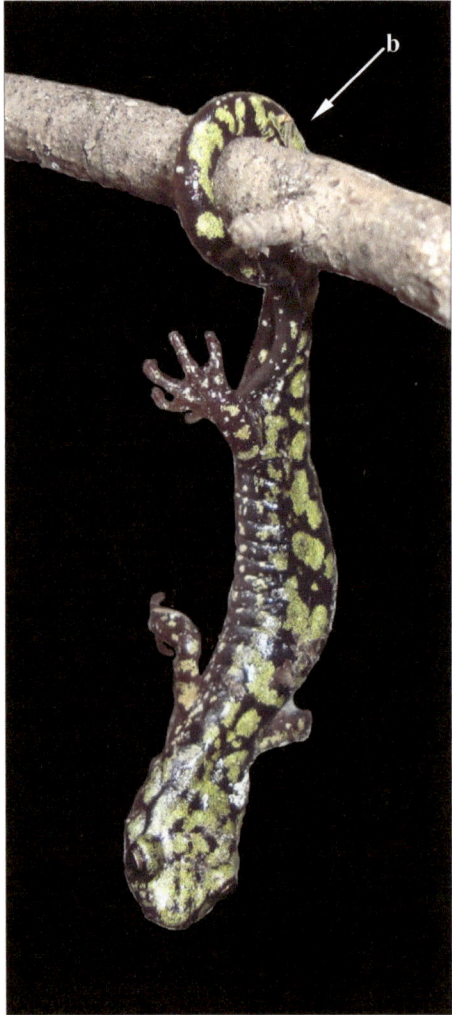

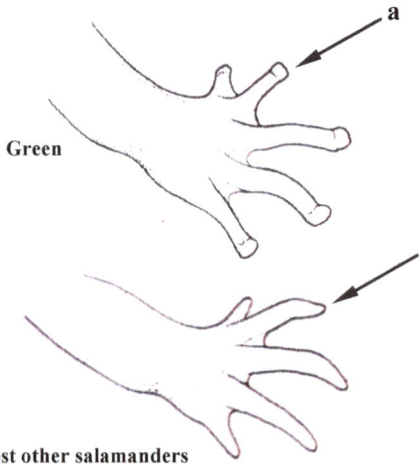

Green

a

Most other salamanders

Green Salamander

Note the lichen pattern on the head and body of the Green Salamander which helps it blend with the whitish-lichens growing on the rock above.

Green Salamander

Note the flattened head for squeezing into tight crevices

Female with eggs

43

Green Salamander

Considered apex predators of sandstone cliffs, Green Salamanders consume a wide range of invertebrates including spiders, snails, and silverfish.

Cave Salamander

Cave Salamander, *Eurycea lucifuga.* (4-6 inches). A thin salamander found in and around the entrances of limestone caves but not considered a true troglobitic (cave) species. Eggs are laid singly and attached by a stalk to sides of small rimstone pools in caves. Larvae live in small surface streams, spring pools, seeps, and underground streams feeding on snails, spiders, copepods, isopods, and many other cave invertebrates. (CP,KN,OB, infrequent in RRG, Natural Bridge Cave, Powell Co, KY).

Chin whitish

Long-tailed Salamander

Vertical tail bars –Long-tailed

Spotted tail–Cave

Tail very long

Pale yellow chin

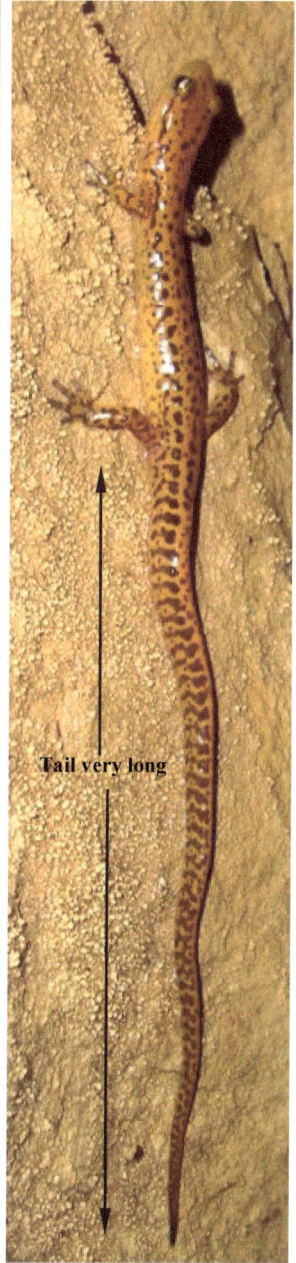

Note vertical bars on tail

Long-tailed Salamander, *Eurycea longicauda.* (4-6 inches). A thin salamander of limestone or sandstone crevices but also found wandering the forest floor on rainy nights. Similar to Cave Salamander but has vertical tail bars (Cave Salamander has spots, see above tail comparison) and a pale yellow chin and belly (Cave Salamander has a whitish chin). Both species can be found at cave entrances. The larvae live in small to large streams, spring pools, and seeps. (CP,KN,OB, common, RRG, Powell Co, KY).

Southern Two-lined Salamander

Southern Two-lined Salamander, *Eurycea cirrigera*. (2-4 inches). A species of small woodland streams throughout most of the year unless it is very cold, the Southern Two-lined is also found on wet roads but becomes more fossorial during the hottest months of summer. Eggs are attached to the undersides of rocks in streams; larvae live in slow-moving pools in same location (opposite page). Note the long, continuous dark line from eye to tail. (CP,KN,OB, common, all images from Martins Fork, RRG, Powell Co, Kentucky).

Southern Two-lined Salamander

Eggs are laid under rocks in streams, which females guard from potential predators

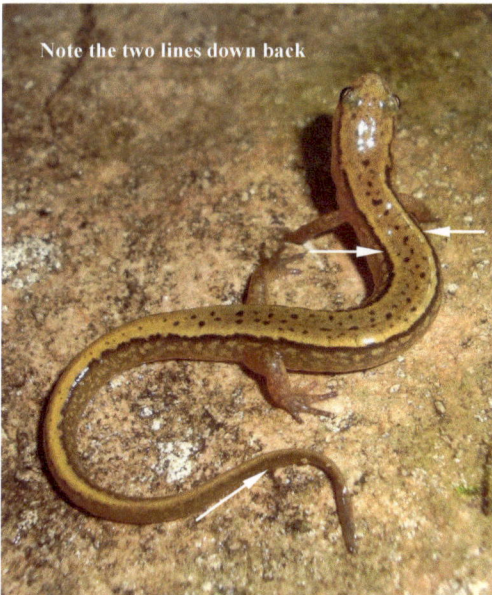

Note the two lines down back

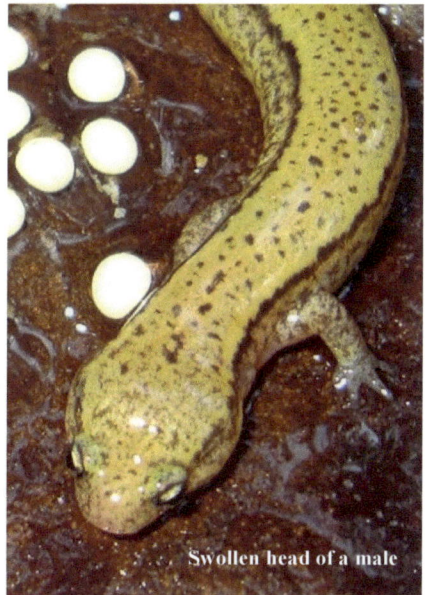

Swollen head of a male

Southern Ravine Salamander

Darker color morph

Southern Ravine Salamander, *Plethodon richmondi.* (3-4 inches). Color variable. Dorsal with gold flecks but hard to see in darker individuals. In early spring, the Southern Ravine Salamander hides under logs, rocks, and in deep leaf litter. During hot summer months, it goes deeper into subterranean regions of the soil. Eggs are laid in underground passageways as with many other salamanders. There is no aquatic stage. Tail thick, long and roundish. (CP,KN,OB, common, RRG, Powell Co, KY).

Northern Zigzag Salamander (not confirmed from Red River Basin)

Northern Zigzag Salamander, *Plethodon dorsalis.* (2-3 inches). A species of rich lime-stone woodlands, residing under logs, rocks, and moist leaf litter. Eggs are laid in deep underground hideaways (Petranka 1998). No aquatic stage. Note the zigzag band down back (a). Although Zigzag Salamanders have not been documented in the Red River watershed, they are known to occur within a few miles of the basin. (OB, Winston near HY 52, Estill County, KY).

Northern Slimy Salamander

White dorsal spots usually large, head thick

Northern Slimy Salamander, *Plethodon glutinosus.* (4-6 inches). A species of rich woodlands, limestone cliffs, and caves, it has large white spots on a dark background. When handled roughly, they produce copious amounts of an adhesive-like secretion from their skin that is water insoluble and not easily removed. Eggs laid in moist places such as logs, under rocks, and occasionally in caves. There is no aquatic stage as in other salamanders. (CP,KN,OB, common, Martins Fork, RRG, Powell Co, KY).

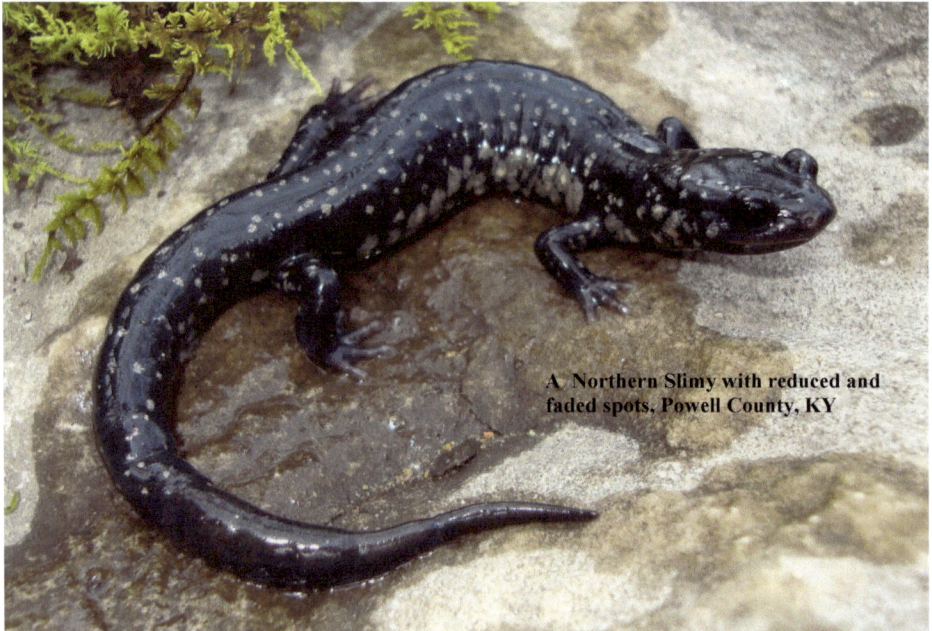

A Northern Slimy with reduced and faded spots, Powell County, KY

Cumberland Plateau Salamander

White dorsal spots small, head thin

Dark chin, Slimy, RRG

Light chin, Cumberland Plateau, RRG

Cumberland Plateau Salamander, *Plethodon kentucki.* (4-6 inches). Similar to the Northern Slimy Salamander but with a lighter chin, thinner head, and smaller dorsal spots. (Slimy has both larger and smaller dorsal spots). A recent study at Lilley Cornett Woods in Letcher Co. Kentucky found 75% of the salamander's diet included ants, spiders, beetles, and springtails with 25% consisting of land snails (Hutton 2017). (CP, infrequent, Little Amos Cave area, Indian Creek, Powell Co, KY).

Seal Salamander

Seal Salamander, *Desmognathus monticola.* (3-6 inches). A variable species of streams, wet sandstone and limestone cliff faces. The Seal has a thin tail (a), plain-colored belly, and dark toe tips or friction pads (b). The Black Mountain also has black toe tips but a heavily-mottled belly. The Seal Salamander and Northern Dusky usually have clear tiny white spots, low along the sides while the Black Mountain does not. Eggs laid in dripping sandstone crevices, bathed in water but never submerged; guarded by the female. All *Desmognathus* (dusky) salamanders possess a light, diagonal line beginning at the eye (c), a feature sometimes difficult to detect. (CP,KN, common, all RRG, Powell Co, KY).

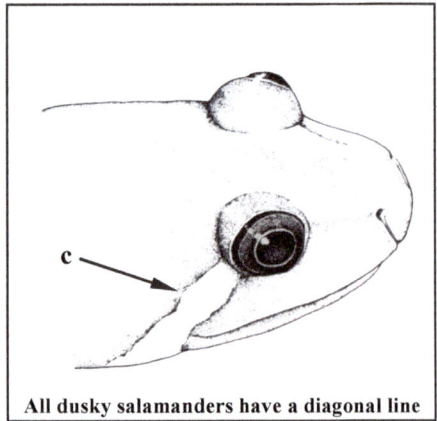

All dusky salamanders have a diagonal line

53

Seal Salamander

An interesting light color morph, RRG

Seal Salamander with eggs, RRG

John MacGregor

Black Mountain Salamander

Black Mountain Salamander, *Desmognathus welteri.* (3-6 inches). A semi-aquatic salamander of cold streams with large rocks and boulders in either limestone or sandstone substrates. This species has dark toe tips (a) and a squared snout. Similar to the Seal Salamander but with a shorter, thicker tail tip. Eggs laid under rocks or moss near the edge of the stream bed, or in damp leaf packs. Larvae live in still pools of same stream. (CP, infrequent, Whittleton Branch, Natural Bridge State Park, Powell Co, KY).

Black Mountain Salamander Habitat

Cool mountain streams bordered by moss-covered rocks are ideal places to find *Desmognathus* species such as the Black Mountain Salamander.

Northern Dusky Salamander

Tail keeled

a

Northern Dusky Salamander, *Desmognathus fuscus.* (2-4 inches). A semi-aquatic salamander of rocky stream banks, and seasonally dry stream beds with rock structure. Similar to the Seal Salamander and Black Mountain Salamander but with clear not dark toe tips (a). Tail keeled. Eggs laid under rocks, moss, or gravel near small streams, where larvae live and feed on small prey such as pea clams, copepods, and water mites. (CP,KN, common, RRG, Powell Co, KY).

Juvenile Northern Dusky

Allegheny Mountain Dusky Salamander

Tail roundish

a

Allegheny Mountain Dusky Salamander, *Desmognathus ochrophaeus.* (2-3 inches). The smallest and most terrestrial of the four Dusky Salamanders in RRG, Allegheny Mountain Dusky salamanders live around seeps, damp rock outcrops, and hillsides close to cool, well-shaded streams. Color variable. Toe tips clear (a). Similar to Northern Dusky but with a round tail, not keeled. Differs from Southern Two-lined Salamander by a light diagonal line from eye and longer snout. Little is known about the larvae of this species. (CP, infrequent, all specimens from Gritter Ridge, Powell Co, KY).

Eastern Hellbender

A flat head helps keep the salamander on the bottom of the river when moving through rapids.

Mark Gumbert, Licking River, KY

Eastern Hellbender

John MacGregor, Licking River, Nicholas Co, KY

Eastern Hellbender, *Cryptobranchus alleganiensis.* (12-24 inches, record 29 inches). A gigantic river salamander living among and under boulders where it hunts its favorite food—soft-shelled crayfish. The many folds of loose skin (a) aid in oxygen absorption. Fossil records of these magnificent animals date back some 65 million years but human habitation of the Red River Basin has managed to push the species to near extirpation from the Red River in less than a century. A river devoid of such extraordinary creatures will indeed be a sad day but perhaps more concerning—a harbinger of what is to come. (CP,KN,OB rare, Licking River, Nicholas Co, KY).

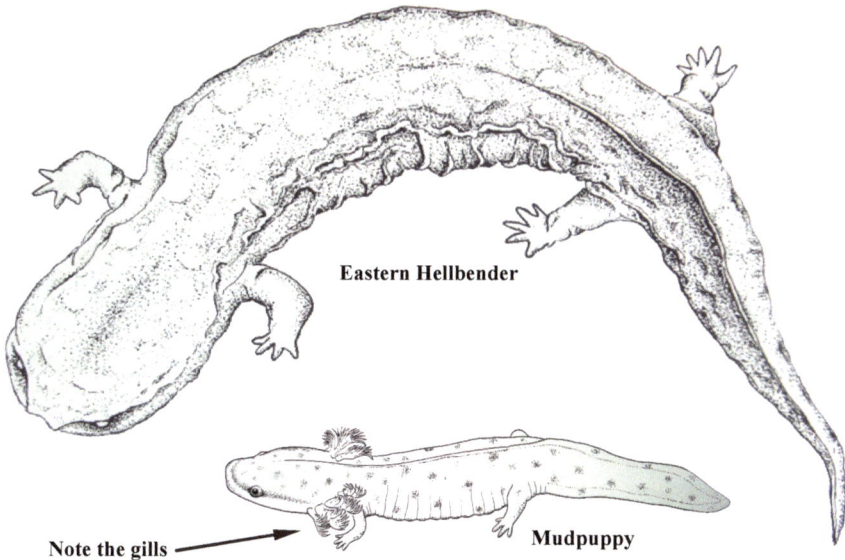

Eastern Hellbender

Note the gills → Mudpuppy

The two large salamanders found in the Red River compared (proportionate)

60

Mudpuppy

Adult

Juveniles have bold stripes

John MacGregor

Mudpuppy, *Necturus maculosus.* (8-19 inches). A robust, aquatic salamander of rivers, the Mudpuppy hides under large rocks during daylight hours becoming a nocturnal hunter after sunset. Adults and larvae feed on a wide range of food including crayfish, snails, a wide range of aquatic invertebrates, and small fish. Mudpuppies are the only species in the basin to retain their gills throughout life and the only known host for the rare Salamander Mussel found in the Red River. Like the Eastern Hellbender, Mudpuppies are becoming increasingly uncommon in the Red River due to water pollution and siltation. (CP,KN,OB, uncommon, top image from Kentucky River & juvenile from Red River, Wolfe Co, KY).

Note the red feathery gills

Mark Gumbert

What do screech owls have to do with a herpetology book? It turns out that in addition to a diet of small mammals, insects, snails, earthworms, spiders, and crayfish, this pintsize owl also feeds on frogs, salamanders, snakes, and lizards—everything in this book except turtles.

Two Salamander Egg Predators

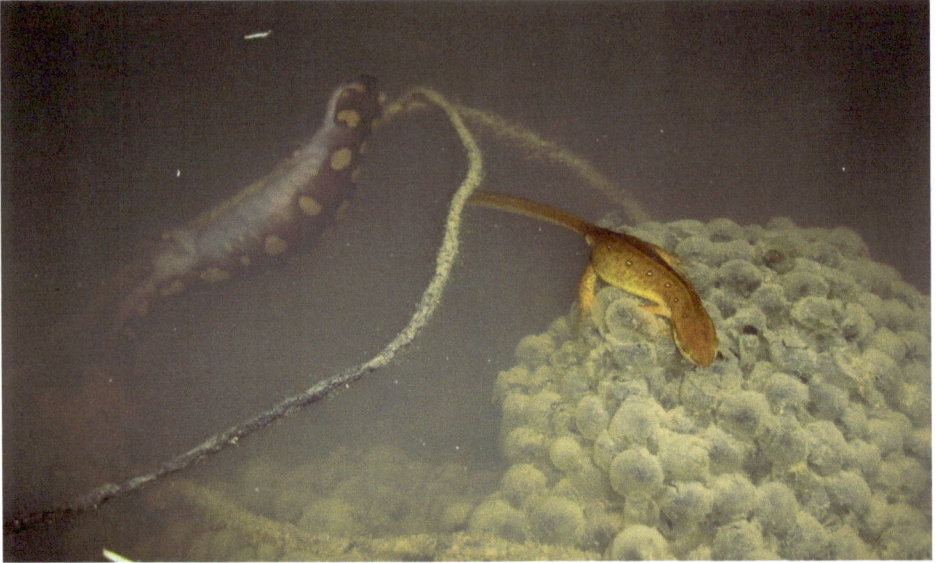

In a quiet little backwoods pond of Red River Gorge, a life and death scenario unfolds (above image). While a Eastern Newt feeds on Wood Frog eggs, a female Spotted Salamander is laying eggs, unbeknownst to her, a voracious predator of her offspring is just inches away. As nature would have it, however, more eggs are laid than will ever hatch—survival by overproduction.

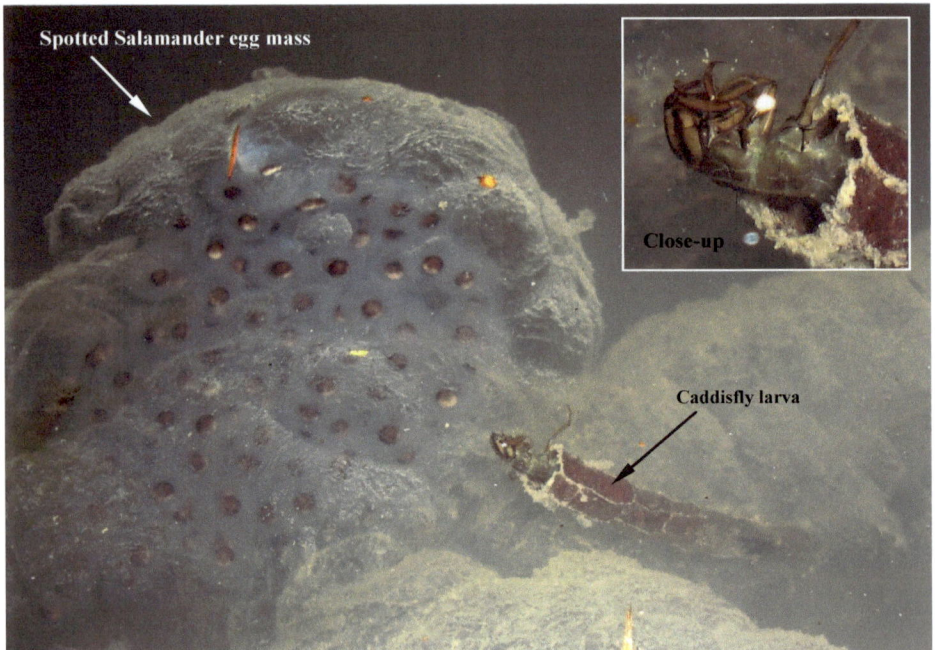

Another voracious predator on the eggs of frogs and salamanders is the caddisfly larva. Above a caddisfly larva digs its way through the protective gel to feed on the protein-rich egg of the Spotted Salamander.

Anurans (Frogs and Toads)

Springtime is a wonderful time in Red River Gorge. The sights, sounds, and smells fill one's senses. If not a hillside covered in white trilliums, it is a symphony of Spring Peepers, Mountain Chorus Frogs, and American Toads. More often heard than seen, Anurans rule the night sounds with their captivating calls. Although the beckoning songs of mating are usually within ear shot of most campsites, few notice this grand old opera, a million years in the making. The size of a frog can be ascertained by the pitch of the call—smaller frogs having higher pitched songs and larger frogs having deep voices. At least 14 species of Anurans are known from the Red River Basin and found in all habitats including limestone caves.

All Anurans in this region lay their eggs in water. Amplexing or mating is the act where usually smaller males sit on top of females (page 70). Males fertilize eggs as they are expelled from females. Eggs hatch into tadpoles and eventually transform or metamorphose into frogs or toads. Tadpoles feed on green algae while frogs feed on just about anything that fits in their over-sized mouths including insects, crayfish, other frogs, and even small mammals such as bats and mice. As nature would have it, Anurans are consumed by nearly anything that can catch them—from snakes to raccoons to birds of prey such as hawks and owls. Consequently, Anurans are an important food source for many local species, keeping the web of life functioning properly. <u>But many frogs and toads are in trouble</u>! In the past three decades, population declines and extinctions of amphibians have occurred worldwide, suffering greater losses than any other group of organisms. Fully one third of the world's 6,260 amphibian species are globally threatened or have gone the way of the dinosaurs. Many scientists believe amphibians serve as warning signs and declines in amphibian populations are early symptoms of an ailing planet.

Research has shown that Anuran declines across the globe have been linked to several important factors; the first and foremost is habitat loss. In most regions of the world, upwards of 95 % of natural wetlands have been drained, paved over or poisoned by human development. This has pushed many species of frogs and toads to the brink of extinction and beyond. A second—and just as concerning mechanism for Anuran die-off—is a fungus belonging to the family of saprobes known as Chytrid disease. Chytrid is caused by the bacteria *Batrachochytrium dendrobatidis,* killing numerous frog and toad species by changing water and salt balances, skin loss and eventually heart failure. First observed in the 1960's, Chytrid fungus has been spreading among amphibian populations throughout the world. The origins of Chytrid was traced to the Korean Peninsula during a 2018 study, spreading through global shipping and the pet trade. But there are apparently multiple strains of Chytrid, and some occur naturally and appear to cause no harm at all. The future consequence of habitat loss, certain strains of Chytrid disease and climate change for amphibians is indeed a bleak one and a reminder of our poor stewardship of the Earth!

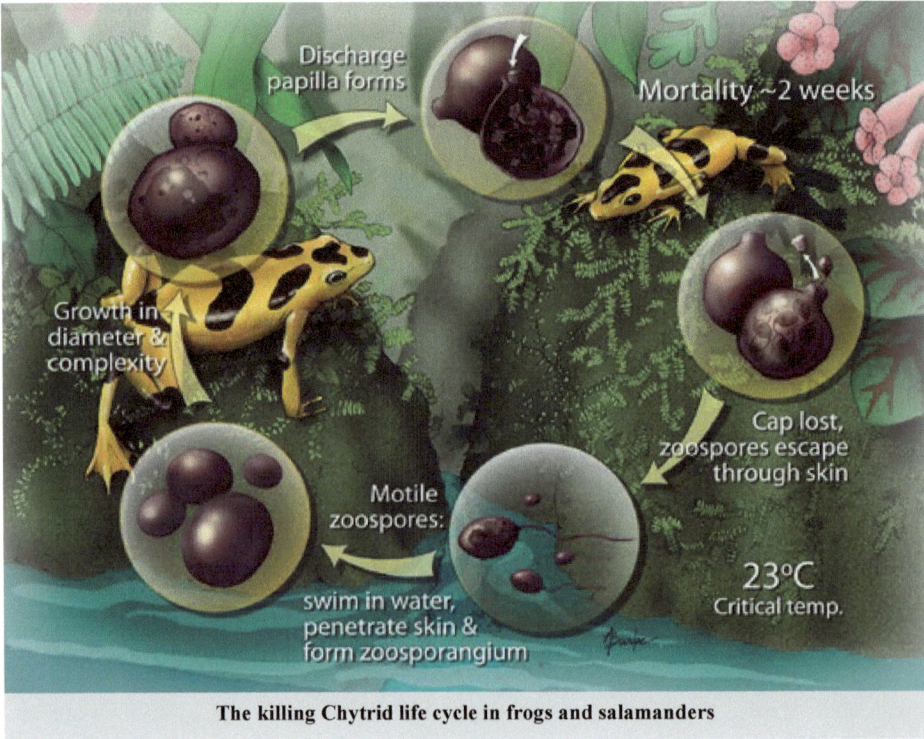

The killing Chytrid life cycle in frogs and salamanders

65

Poison dart frog from Peru

Although not nearly as toxic or colorful as the poison dart frogs of Central and South America (above), Anurans in Kentucky do contain noxious skin secretions and are marked with contrasting colors to warn of their distasteful compounds.

Five Tiny Frogs Compared

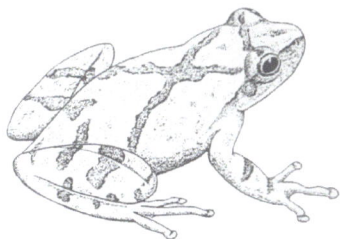

Spring Peeper (X stripe)

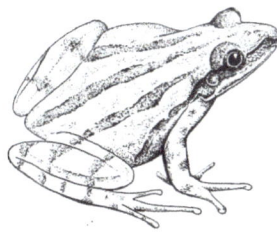

Upland Chorus (3 stripes)

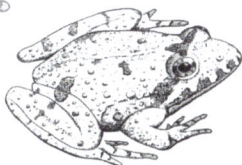

Blanchard's Cricket Frog (warty skin)

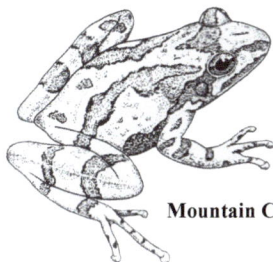

Mountain Chorus (2 stripes)

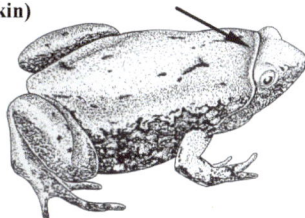

Narrow-mouthed Toad (skin fold overhead)

American Bullfrog

a

Tympanum

A spotted color morph

American Bullfrog, *Lithobates catesbeianus.* (4-8 inches). A giant among Anurans, American Bullfrogs live in large and small ponds, old oxbows, sloughs, and along rivers. During breeding season, the male frogs call with their loud and cavernous voices. Similar to the smaller Green Frog but the dorsolateral fold (a) wraps around the tympanum instead of extending down its back like the Green Frog. If you have ever eaten frog legs, it was most likely this species. (CP,KN,OB, summer, common, Powell Co, KY).

Green Frog

A Green Frog with unusual spotting

Green Frog, *Lithobates clamitans.* (3-4 inches). A medium-sized frog of ponds, ditches, oxbows, and small streams. Calls of the male Green Frog sound similar to a breaking banjo string. As in most frogs, the diet includes just about anything that will fit in the frog's over-sized mouth. Breeding males have bright yellow throats. Similar to the American Bullfrog but the dorsolateral fold extends down the back (a) and to a lesser degree, around the tympanum. (CP,KN,OB, summer, common, Powell Co, KY).

Wood Frog

Wood Frog, *Lithobates sylvaticus.* (2-3 inches). A late winter/early spring breeder, Wood Frogs have been referred to as "antifreeze frogs", a result of their ability to fully function in freezing weather. In fact, these Anurans are so durable that they have been observed jumping, calling, and laying eggs amidst falling snow. While in hibernation, Wood Frogs can tolerate blood and other body tissues freezing solid due to the production of urea and glucose which act as cryoprotectants that limit ice buildup—thus reducing osmotic shrinkage of cells (Storey 1985). Wood Frogs have characteristic dark masks around the eyes and breed in small fishless ponds. A chorus of Wood Frogs sounds a bit like squabbling ducks. Also known to chorus during cool fall nights. (CP,KN, calls mid winter to early spring and in fall, common, all images RRG, Powell Co, KY).

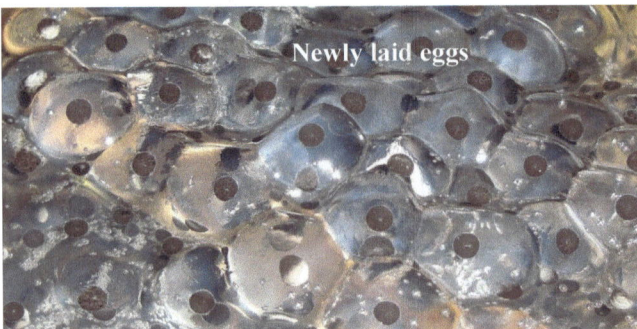

Newly laid eggs

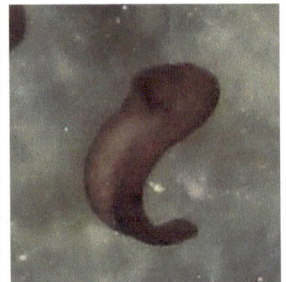

A developing larva

Amplexing Wood Frogs

Amplexing Wood Frogs with the larger, lighter female on bottom, Cane Creek, Powell Co, KY

Amplexing Wood Frogs with the smaller, darker male on top, Cane Creek, Powell Co, KY

70

Pickerel Frog

A live Pickerel Frog showing the yellow undersides of its legs

Pickerel Frog, *Lithobates palustris.* (2-3 inches). This beautiful frog is a common species of wetlands but also found deep in limestone caves especially during winter and hot summer months. The undersides of legs and sides are yellowish (Leopards Frogs are without yellow undersides). Eggs are laid in ponds. Pickerel Frogs emit strong skin secretions which are irritating to people and toxic to some predators. Calls are low and nasal. (CP,KN,OB, calls in late spring early summer, common, RRG, Powell Co, KY).

Northern Leopard Frog

John MacGregor, Franklin County, Kentucky

Northern Leopard Frog, *Lithobates pipiens* (3-4 inches). Separated from Southern Leopard Frog by the following characters: adult Southern Leopard Frogs almost always have an obvious white dot in the center of the tympanum and have a more slender build, lighter bars on the femur, slightly narrower and more delicate dorsolateral folds, and slightly longer snouts. Northern Leopard Frogs never have the white dot in the eardrum but some can have a light-colored circular area there. They tend to be bulkier frogs with heavy bars on the femur, and less sharply pointed snouts. With or without a dark snout spot. Color variable. Habitat similar to Southern Leopard Frog. Calls are a low, quiet, deep, rattling snore followed by a chuckle. (CP,KN,OB, calls in early spring, occurrence poorly known in watershed, bottom image questionable Northern Leopard Frog from Powell Co, KY).

Les Meade, (2008) Cane Creek, Powell Co, Kentucky

Southern Leopard Frog

Powell Co, KY

Southern Leopard Frog, *Lithobates sphenocephalus* (3-4 inches). A species of open and wooded floodplains of the Red River Basin, mostly around Clay City and Stanton. Breeds in wet depressions and ponds. Dorsolateral fold distinctive from eye to hind leg. Similar to Pickerel Frog but lacking the bright yellow color located under the hind leg (seen on the Pickerel Frog), having a light spot in the tympanum (absent on the Pickerel Frog). Southern Leopard Frog has more rounded spots while Pickerel Frogs have spots that are more squared or rectangular in shape, although this feature is variable. Northern Leopard Frog has a blunter snout and lacks a well defined dot in the eardrum. As in most frogs, tadpoles graze on algae while adults are carnivorous—eating just about anything that the frog can overpower. Calls sound like chuckling ducks. Images here of a male in full breading colors.(CP,KN,OB, calls in early spring, infrequent, flooded fields around Stanton and Clay City, both images taken near Stanton, Powell Co, KY).

Powell Co, Kentucky

Three Similar *Lithobates* Species Compared

Pickerel Frog

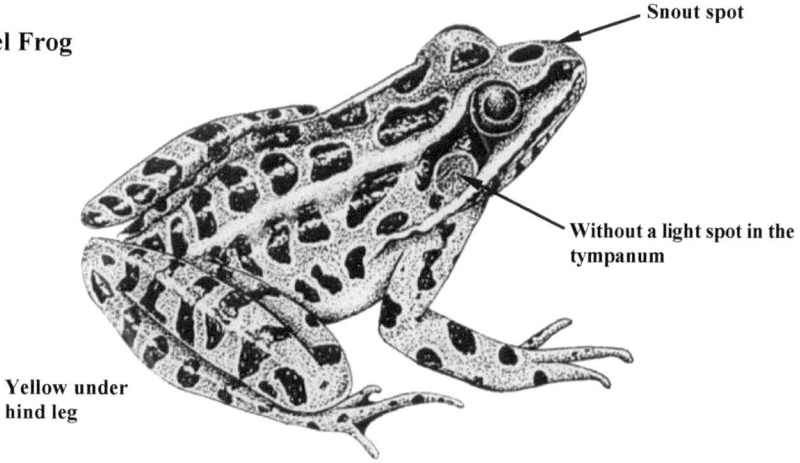

Snout spot

Without a light spot in the tympanum

Yellow under hind leg

Southern Leopard Frog

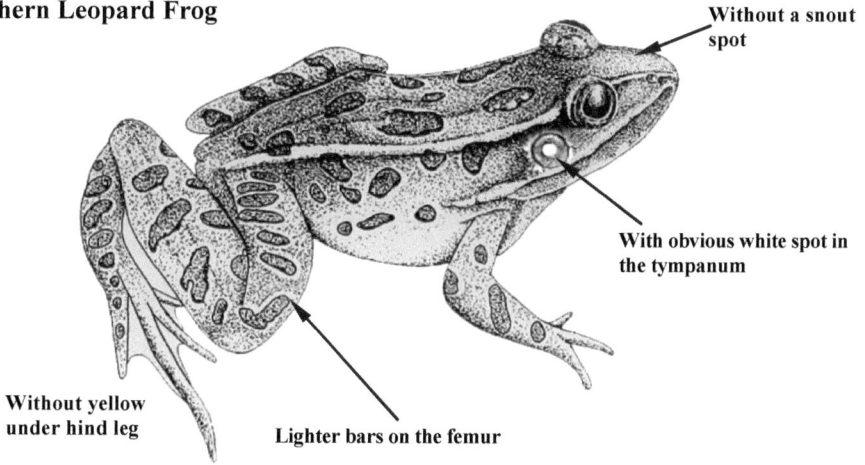

Without a snout spot

With obvious white spot in the tympanum

Without yellow under hind leg

Lighter bars on the femur

Northern Leopard Frog

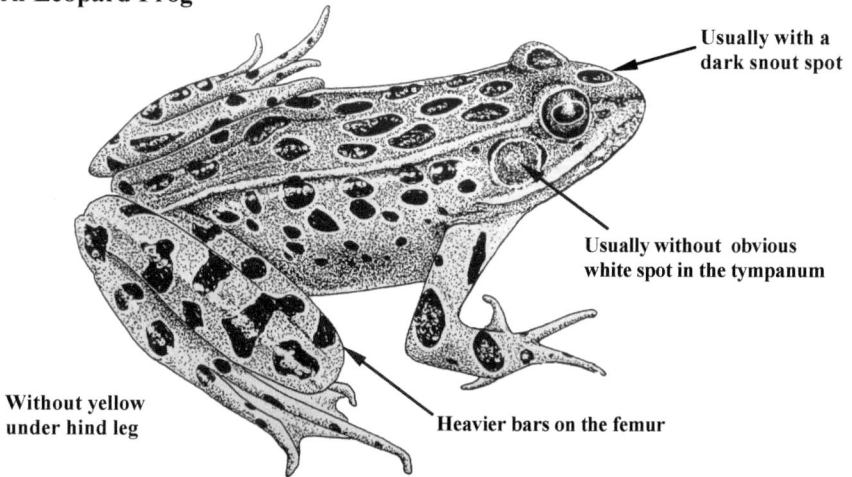

Usually with a dark snout spot

Usually without obvious white spot in the tympanum

Without yellow under hind leg

Heavier bars on the femur

American Toad

American Toad, *Anaxyrus americanus.* (2-4 inches). A familiar toad found just about everywhere from bottomlands to ridgetops. Breeds in early spring during heavy rains. The beautiful, necklace-like eggs are deposited in open sunny ditches and ponds. Hind feet are equipped with digging spurs. Calls of the American Toad are bird-like trills and pleasing to the ear. Contrary to popular belief, toads do not give you warts. (CP,KN,OB, calls in early spring, common, Cane Creek, Powell Co, KY).

A calling American Toad

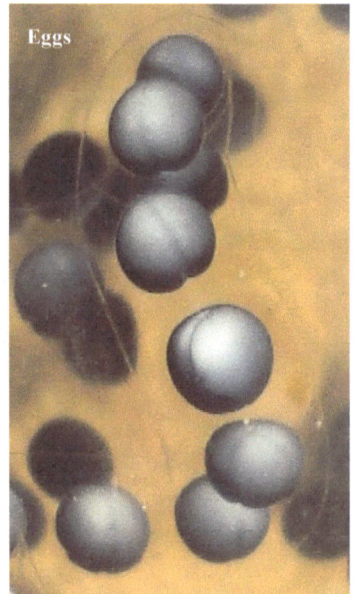

Eggs

Fowler's Toad

Fowler's Toad, *Anaxyrus fowleri.* (2-3 inches). A species of both floodplains and uplands, breeding in late spring during heavy rains in the shallows of lakes, large ponds, and sluggish shallow open sections of streams. Similar to American Toad but having three or more warts contained within some dark spots (American Toads usually contain 1-2 warts per dark spot). (a & b). Calls are a nasal trill. (CP,KN,OB, calls in late spring, common, Lulbegrud Creek, Clark Co, KY).

Eastern Spadefoot Toad

Eastern Spadefoot, *Scaphiopus holbrookii.* (2-3 inches). A burrowing Anuran of sandy soils, the Spadefoot Toad is rarely seen except during its brief, explosive breeding after heavy downpours and loud thunder. Breeding in Kentucky can occur in any month of the year but typically during mid-spring to early summer. Eggs are laid in natural ridgetop ponds but also known to breed in bottomland floodplains of the Red River around Clay City and Stanton. Calls are nasal and travel a long distance. Like toads, the hind feet of Spadefoots are equipped with digging spurs (a) used to burrow backwards. The only Anuran in Kentucky with elliptical pupils (opposite page). Diet includes invertebrates, insects, arachnids, termites, worms, and larvae of several insect species. (CP,KN, infrequent, Stanton, Powell Co, KY).

Eastern Spadefoot Toad

Elliptical eyes of gold

Eastern Spadefoot Toad

Defensive posture

2 color morphs (dorsal view)

79

Eastern Spadefoot Toad

Spadefoot Yoga, the lotus position

Cope's Gray Treefrog

Cope's Gray Treefrog, *Hyla chrysoscelis.* (1-2 inches). Treefrogs are unlike most species of frogs, spending the majority of their time in lofty vegetation such as trees. As a result, treefrogs are rarely encountered except during stormy summer months when treefrogs are close to or in breeding pools. Here, they are easily observed calling, amplexing, or laying eggs. Treefrogs have warty skin and expanded toe pads (a) for climbing and are a variable species in terms of color and patterns. Metamorphosing treefrogs are gold with stumpy tails (b) which soon disappear. Calls are loud, raspy, and short. Figure (c) depicts a water strider feeding on treefrog eggs. (CP,KN,OB, calls in summer, common, all images from Martins Fork, RRG, Powell Co, KY).

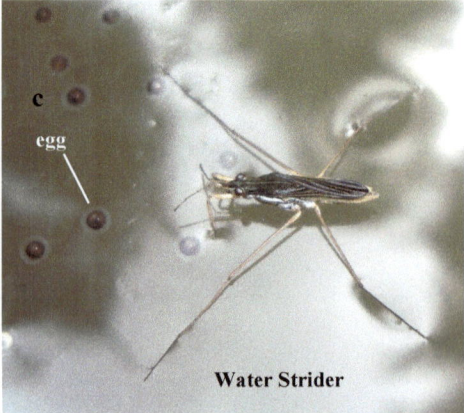

Cope's Gray Treefrog

Above image of an inflated vocal sac of a calling Cope's Gray Treefrog, RRG, KY

Dexterous hands

Hind legs of Cope's Gray Treefrog are bright yellow and spotted

Spring Peeper, *Pseudacris crucifer.* (1 inch). While the calls of Spring Peepers are pleasing to the ear from a distance, in the midst of many, eardrums are pushed to decibel limits! Their high piercing calls are a result of the large vocal sac, acting as a voice amplifier. Males call nearly every night from March-June and pairs in amplexus can be found in all kinds of weather. In fall, calls are limited to short chirps. The best distinguishing feature is the "X" marking on the back (a). (CP,KN,OB, calls in early spring, common, Gritter Ridge, Powell Co, KY).

Spring Peeper

The large inflated vocal sac of a calling male Spring Peeper

Mountain Chorus Frog

Mountain Chorus Frog, *Pseudacris brachyphona.* (1 inch). A small treefrog of upland sites, breeding in small, very temporary pools containing little water. In fact, these frogs will lay snot-like egg masses in nothing more than a puddle. Calls are a nasal "reek-reek". Similar to Spring Peeper in size but having 2 light or dark dorsal stripes that bend toward the center. Spring Peepers have dorsal stripes forming an "X" on the back (page 66). (CP,KN, calls in early spring, common, Cane Creek, Powell Co, KY).

Egg mass

Upland Chorus Frog (not confirmed from Red River Basin)

Upland Chorus Frog, *Pseudacris feriarum.* A small treefrog of lowlands, breeding and laying eggs in flooded farmland and other wide open wetlands. Calls sound like a person running a fingernail over a comb but much louder. Although the species is not yet documented from the Red River watershed, there are several close populations around the town of Irvine on the north side of the Kentucky River (KN,OB, calls in late winter to early spring, images from Grayson Co, KY).

Egg laid on a blade of submerged grass

Blanchard's Cricket Frog

Blanchard's Cricket Frog, *Acris blanchardi.* (1 inch). One of the smallest Anurans occurring in the Basin (around the size of a quarter), Blanchard's Cricket Frogs can be found adjacent to ponds and other wetlands around Clay City. Calls sound like hitting two small stones together. Breeding takes place in ponds. With or without neon-green markings on back. Surface of the frog is warty. Tadpoles have a distinctive black-tipped tail. (KN,OB, calls in summer, infrequent, both images from Pine Ridge Road, Clark Co, KY).

Eastern Narrow-mouthed Toad (Introduced)

Eastern Narrow-mouthed Toad, *Gastrophryne carolinensis.* (1 inch). A small Anuran of floodplains, breeding in small, very temporary pools containing little water. Calls are a nasal tone lasting a few seconds. There is a characteristic fold of skin covering a portion of the head. Eastern Narrow-mouthed Toad tadpoles from around Somerset, Kentucky were introduced to the Upper Cane Creek watershed, Powell County in 2001. Calling and amplexing Narrow-mouthed Toads were observed by the authors at this location in May 10, 2015 and May 26, 2017. (both images from Cane Creek population, rare, Powell County, KY). Refer to page 66 for 5 tiny frog comparisons.

Not a cobra but a marvelously evolved serpent known as the Eastern Hog-nosed Snake. This animal has developed some rather bizarre and clever strategies to stay alive.

Snakes

No other group of animals provokes such widespread panic and fear in humans as do snakes. The fear of snakes is called ophidiophobia.

Known since biblical times as the spreader of sinful deeds, snakes in truth are bringers of balance and are among the most highly engineered hunters on Earth! Slender, limbless, and flexible bodies allow snakes to hunt in places like small round burrows that would leave a cat panting for a rat. Snakes directly help maintain natural trophic interactions and indirectly, affect public health by reducing famine and disease. For example, the principal mammal vectors of the *Borrelia* bacteria causing Lyme Disease is found in Eastern Chipmunks and White-footed Mice. Healthy, intact carnivore communities including bobcats, foxes, raccoons, opossums, owls, hawks, and snakes which control rodent populations have been shown to suppress infections in ticks, in turn, reducing human exposure to Lyme. The mass killing of snakes—rattlesnake roundups popular in western United States—has likely influenced ecosystems that may change predator-prey population dynamics. High levels of human-caused mortality of snakes correlates to an increase in rodent populations, reducing cereal grain production while increasing the risk of diseases such as Hantavirus.

Numerous native snakes are in danger of disappearing forever, and while many would lose little sleep over the loss of serpents, ecosystems would suffer immensely. According to the Royal Society, snake populations worldwide are declining at unprecedented rates from gratuitous killing and habitat loss (Reading et al. 2010). Another concerning threat to snakes is a fungus called *Ophidiomyces ophiodiicola*. The fungus can cause severe skin lesions in at least 14 species of snakes and mortality rates can be as high as 90 percent (Clark et al. 2010; Rajeev et al. 2009).

Of the 18 species of serpents known from the watershed, only two species, the Copperhead and Rattlesnake, contain venom (not poison) strong enough to be injurious to humans. Furthermore, contrary to public perception, neither of these snakes are known to be aggressive unless molested. Most remain tranquil or simply move away. People insist that Copperheads are antagonistic animals, confusing a defensive behavior (sitting in place and striking at an intruder) with an aggressive behavior (chasing the intruder and biting). Few snakes will ever chase a threat to their lives!

In the past, snakes have been categorized as either venomous or non-venomous. In reality, there's a whole group of snakes in between—containing slightly reactive saliva—referred to as opisthoglyphous (meaning rear-fanged). The Eastern Hog-nosed Snake (image below) has 2 sharp fangs that are used to puncture the tough hide of a toad where it introduces a mild venom, subduing the toad for consumption. Two other rear-fanged snakes in the RRG include the Ring-necked and Common Wormsnake. All opisthoglyphous snakes in the US are considered harmless to humans.

The rear fang of an Eastern Hog-nosed Snake, Powell County, Kentucky

A Red-bellied Snake using its tongue to smell its surroundings, RRG, KY

The tongue of a snake picks up scent particles which are transferred to the Jacobson's-organ located on the roof of the snake's mouth where it is analyzed for chemical content. The nasal passageway of a snake is also used to sample volatile odors. While the snake's sense of smell is excellent, its sense of hearing is a different story. Snakes are without eardrums but they still possess inner ears. Research has shown that snakes respond to vibrational stimuli that occur on the ground, air or even through water. So the popular notion that snakes are deaf is not exactly true, although their hearing is restricted to a limited range of sound frequencies from approximately 50-1000 Hz (Lillywhite 2014). While snakes might hear a stampede of box turtles coming, the high-pitched screams of a panic-stricken human will likely go unnoticed.

When snakes are ready to shed, a fluid from the lymphatic system spreads under the skin, separating the old skin from the new, giving the snake a gray or bluish cast. There is a local myth that snakes go blind during the dog days of August. But snakes can shed at any-time during spring, summer, or fall and healthy snakes shed more often than poorly fed ones. Furthermore, snakes during this time may be more irritable, a result of being nearly blind by the opaque condition of their eyes (image to the right of an opaque eye).

A Gray Ratsnake with an opaque eye, RRG, KY

92

20 Common Snake Myths

1. **Copperheads smell like cucumbers.** Cucumber smell has been wrongly associated with the presence of Copperheads, the odor more than likely the musk of a nearby short-tailed shrew or rotting fungi (pers. comm. John MacGregor, 2016).
2. **A snake must coil before a strike.** While a snake can bite from any position, a coiled snake has the advantage of being able to strike farther (typically one third its body length).
3. **Milksnakes and cowsuckers (Ratsnakes) milk cows.** Nope! Can you image a snake with a mouth full of needle-sharp teeth latching onto the sensitive teat of a cow? Ouch!
4. **Snakes are slimy.** Snakes actually have very dry skin.
5. **Snakes are poisonous.** Snakes are <u>venomous not poisonous.</u> Venom is a modified saliva.
6. **Rattlesnakes always rattle before they strike.** Not always.
7. **Snakes will grow into separate fully functional individuals when cut into pieces.** This is completely false.
8. **Venomous snake bites are always venomous.** Up to 50% of venomous snake bites to non-prey targets like deer and humans may be dry bites, meaning no venom is injected.
9. **Constrictors asphyxiate their prey.** It turns out that constrictors kill by stopping the prey's blood flow, starving all organs of oxygen, not by suffocation.
10. **Snakes will chase you.** Very rarely. When snakes feel threatened, they employ 3 strategies to stay alive: remain still, flee, or bite—a similar response from most animals including humans. Racers will occasionally chase and bite a perceived threat but most snakes in general bite only as a last resort.
11. **Female Copperheads will swallow their young when danger threatens them.** Because Copperheads have live birth, if a female with babies is killed, live babies may crawl out from the carcass, hence starting this interesting but outrageous myth.
12. **If you are bitten by a Greensnake you will laugh yourself to death.** Anyone who believes this, stand on your head!
13. **Some snakes can sting with their tail.** No snakes have stinging tails.
14. **Hoop snakes can bite their tail and roll down the hill.** Refer to answer #12.
15. **Snakes cannot strike underwater**: Many watersnakes rely on their ability to bite and seize prey underwater.
16. **Black snakes will mate with Copperheads.** This myth most likely comes from an observation made of an all-black Eastern Hog-nosed Snake (page 146) which is often mistaken for a Black Snake mating with a normal color-phase of a Eastern Hog-nosed Snake which is often mistaken for a Copperhead.
17. **Snakes hypnotize their prey.** There is no scientific basis for this silly claim.
18. **Moth balls will keep snakes away.** No, but moth balls are toxic to your pets and wildlife.
19. **Snakes are evil.** Many people believe that snakes are inherently evil, an idea found in no less than 44 Bible verses. Genesis 3:14 states "and the Lord God said to the serpent, Because you have done this, cursed are you more than all cattle, and more than every beast of the field, on your belly you will go, and dust you will eat all the days of your life". Not one snake of the more than 3400 species worldwide eats dust, except inadvertently, as do most other creatures including humans. Snakes, like legless lizards, crawl on their bellies because an appendage-free design was more functional, especially in round holes were rodents live. Clearly, the folks who wrote the Bible had no real love for serpents and little understanding of the irreplaceable importance that snakes have in functioning ecosystems. Snakes are no more evil than puppies.
20. **There are cottonmouths in Eastern Kentucky.** There has never been a cottonmouth confirmed from Red River Gorge or eastern Kentucky (see opposite page). Most sightings are Common Watersnakes (page 139), or some other species.

Cottonmouths DO NOT occur in Eastern Kentucky!

Northern Cottonmouth

Juvenile Cottonmouth

Cottonmouth with gaping white mouth

Range of the Northern Cottonmouth, *Agkistrodon piscivorus* in Kentucky

RRG area

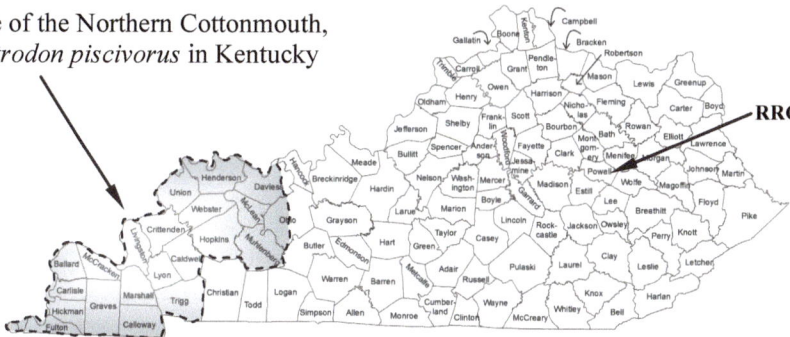

The closest population of the Northern Cottonmouth to Red River Gorge is around 175 miles away in Daviess County, Kentucky.

94

Poisonous or Venomous Snakes?

The term "poisonous" used when referring to snakes is actually misleading. Technically, the substance these snakes possess is a modified saliva called venom used to inject, kill, and digest the snake's prey and to a lesser degree for self-defense.

Venoms are of two basic types: neurotoxin or hemotoxin and sometimes a mixture of the two. Neurotoxins attack and disable the central nervous system, causing the heart and diaphragm muscles to stop working. Hemotoxins target the circulatory system by affecting clotting compounds resulting in uncontrolled bleeding and destroying subcutaneous and muscle tissue on a massive scale. Unlike venom, true poison can kill by simple ingestion. One example, strychnine, is highly toxic to humans and if taken internally can kill within hours. In contrast, venom is generally not dangerous when ingested, having little or no ill effect as long as there are no open sores or ulcers along its path to the stomach where it is neutralized by our stomach's soup of digestive juices.

Some snakes are opisthoglyphous (rear-fanged) and bites from these animals may produce local pain and other symptoms of very mild envenomation (Stafford and Meyer 2000) but are never fatal to humans. The Eastern Hog-nosed Snake is one such species. It has a set of rear fangs located on the upper mandible that is used to infuse a venom into its prey consisting mainly of toads. It was only recently discovered that the saliva of the Common Gartersnake contains a very mild neurotoxin that can cause minor swelling and itching in humans but in frogs or small rodents has a stunning affect—making consumption easier for the snake. Watersnake bites may also cause undesirable reactions due to pathogens found in the mouth from an aquatic lifestyle.

A "dry bite" from a venomous snake is a bite in which no venom is injected. Although widely debated, "dry bites" to non-prey animals such as deer or humans may vary considerably, depending on the species of snake. Bites occurring in the wild appear to be dry bites about 40 to 50 percent of the time with only 5 to 10 percent being severe envenomations (pers. comm. Jim Harrison, 2017). Some research suggests that venomous snakes can and do control the venom flow since making new venom is costly for snakes to manufacture, requiring multiple meals. If a snake were to bite and inject venom into every threatening movement in the woods, the snake would quickly deplete its venom reserves, resulting in a lack of venom when needed to secure a meal.

Dry bites may have started the myth that certain forest plants such as Virginia snakeroot, *Endodeca serpentaria,* can heal snake bites. Native Americans chewed the root and also applied it to wounds but there is no scientific evidence supporting the use of snakeroot to cure snakebite. When promptly treated with anti-venin—the only proven treatment for a venomous snake bite—few people die. In the US, there are an estimated 7,000-8,000 bites from venomous snakes annually resulting in less than 5 deaths per year and nearly all from Rattlesnakes. While a dry bite will exhibit little discomfort, a full envenomation will manifest severe swelling and excruciating pain.

In general, snakes kill food by: 1) grabbing their prey and consuming it alive like the Common Gartersnake 2) seizing and constricting the prey until death like the Eastern Black Kingsnake 3) by hypodermic injection of a lethal dose of saliva or venom like the Copperhead and Rattlesnake. Copperheads and Rattlesnakes are considered two of the more evolved serpents in Kentucky, having highly efficient methods for killing and hunting prey.

This includes copious venom glands connected to enlarged hollow fangs that act as hypodermic needles and the remarkably evolved pit (see diagram below). The pit is a heat-sensing organ that produces a thermal image which enables the snake to track a freshly bitten, warm-blooded animal through dense forests in total darkness.

Much research has been devoted to snake venom with great promise for developing life-saving drugs. Toxic compounds such as anticoagulant, anti-platelet, and anti-hypertensive agents found in venom may yield new drugs to treat everything from crippling strokes to the prevention of cardiovascular and cerebrovascular disease. Neurotoxins present in coral snakes could be used to treat brain injuries, strokes, and Alzheimer's disease while blood thinning compounds found in the venom of the fer-de-lance could be used to treat heart attacks or blood disorders.

French scientists believe one compound from Copperhead venom might be useful in fighting breast cancer. Cobra venom is being investigated for use in treating Parkinson's disease. Research has already resulted in several new drugs based on snake venom compounds including Aggrastat, a "super aspirin" that prevents blood clots. Scientists are only now realizing the potential contributions that venomous snakes will make to humanity—still yet another reason to protect all creatures great and small.

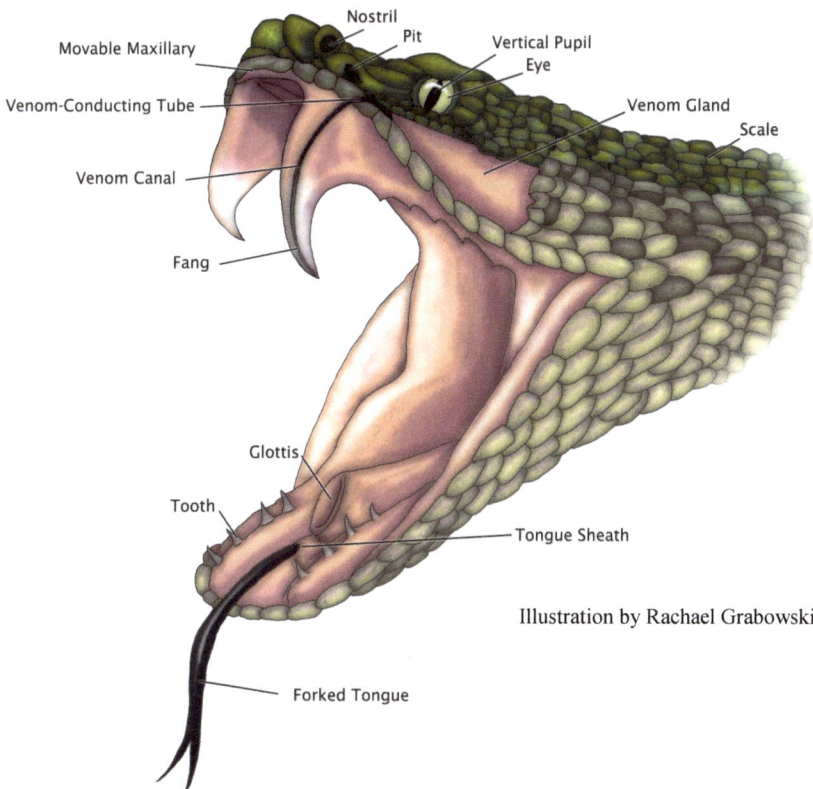

Illustration by Rachael Grabowski

Common Wormsnake

Uncommon lighter color morph

Common Wormsnake, *Carphophis amoenus.* (7-11 inches). This tiny snake looks more like a worm than a snake. It is a burrower but can be found under or inside rotting logs, under rocks, and other cover. If handled by a human, the snake never bites but uses its pointed tail as a defensive apparatus—poking it into the skin with little effect but stuck in the eye of an aggressive shrew—probably agonizing. (CP,KN,OB, common, two color morphs shown, top image, Indian Creek, Powell Co, KY and bottom image, Wolfe/Breathitt County line, KY).

Common Wormsnake

Head narrow; used to burrow in loose soils

Eyes small

Note the pointed tail used as a defensive apparatus against potential predators such as shrews

Smooth Earthsnake

Smooth Earthsnake, *Virginia valeriae.* (12-16 inches). Smooth Earthsnakes are small, secretive snakes of old fields and, like many small snakes are found under just about anything providing some protective cover. The snake will not bite if handled. Similar to Common Wormsnake but with a shorter snout. With or without a double row of dark spots down the back (see above images). Diet includes earthworms as well as soft-bodied insects and their larvae. (CP,KN, rare, upper Cane Creek, Powell Co, KY).

Smooth Earthsnake

An adult Smooth Earthsnake

Dekay's Brownsnake

Dekay's Brownsnake, *Storeria dekayi.* (12-20 inches). A small snake of woodlands and meadows found under just about anything providing some protection. The snake rarely bites when handled. It has a whitish belly (not red as in Red-bellied Snake) and cross markings on the dorsal side (top)—some forming large triangles. Dekay's Brownsnakes feed on a variety of invertebrates including those exotic, pesky garden slugs (pers. comm. John MacGregor, 2016). (CP,KN,OB, common, Powell Co, KY).

Dekay's Brownsnake

Close-up of facial markings

Belly whitish

Red-bellied Snake

Red-bellied Snake, *Storeria occipitomaculata* (12-16 inches). A small snake of wooded edges and openings found under logs, rocks and debris. Diet includes snail and slugs (Red-bellied snakes have special adaptations of their teeth and jaws that allow them to extract snails from their shells, similar to Dekay's Brownsnake), earthworms, and soft-bodied insects. Red-bellied Snakes have 3 light spots on neck, opposite page (figure a and b opposite page); Ring-necked Snakes have a solid yellow band. Dorsal side is somewhat plain but its ventral side or belly ranges from a deep red to pale orange either in a narrow or wide band. Red-bellied Snakes will not bite when handled but usually deposit a smelly musk on a perceived threat (CP,KN,OB, common, images from Powell County, Kentucky).

Juvenile Red-bellied Snake

Red-bellied Snake

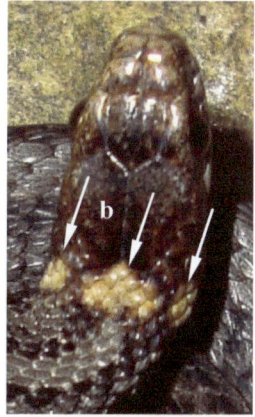

A narrow red belly band

A wide red belly band

Red-bellied Snake (local variation)

Red-bellied Snake Defenses

Snake in a protective posture, with head buried in coil

Red–bellied Snakes are consumed by a number of predators including crows, hawks, screech owls, raccoons, opossums, shrews, and Eastern Milksnakes. Their tiny teeth have little affect on these much larger animals, so the snake has developed several defense tactics to avoid being eaten. A foul-smelling anal secretion may be smeared on the attacker. Some Red-bellied Snakes will stiffen and roll onto their backs when harassed—playing dead, exposing their bright red belly which may startle the predator momentarily, allowing the snake to escape. Red-bellied snakes will also flare their lips exposing their teeth (a).

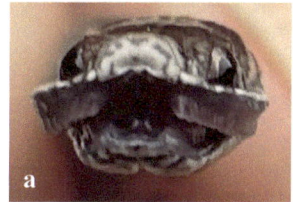

Ring-necked Snake

Dorsal without any patterns

An infrequent spotted belly pattern

Ring-necked Snake, *Diadophis punctatus.* (12-16 inches). A small snake occupying a wide range of habitats, from valley floors to dry, sandstone ridgetops. Ring-necked Snakes have a yellow ring around the neck (a) and a yellow belly (with or without black belly spots). The species is easily found in early to late spring under a variety of protective cover such as rocks, logs, and my personal favorite, old roofing tin. It is not uncommon to find three of four under one piece of metal. Sometimes found with the Red–bellied Snake and Dekay's Brownsnake. Ring-necked Snakes are rear-fanged and mildly venomous, and although the venom is effective on small prey like salamanders, earthworms, and slugs, it is considered completely harmless to humans. (CP,KN,OB, common, all images from Indian Creek area of Powell Co, KY).

Ring-necked Snake

Ring-necked Snakes rarely bite in self-defense, but instead, expose a bright yellow belly and coiled tail (a) as a warning or decoy. While your eyes are being dazzled by bright colors, your nose is being repulsed by the snake's smelly musk just deposited on your hands! As a last resort, the snake conceals its head in a protective coil (below image).

5 Adult Snake Species Under 20 Inches Compared

Common Wormsnake

RRG, Powell Co, KY

Ring-necked Snake

RRG, Powell Co, KY

Smooth Earthsnake

Cane Creek, Powell Co, KY

Red-bellied Snake

Dekay's Brownsnake

6 Juvenile Snakes with Bold Dorsal Patterns Compared

Red Cornsnake

RRG, Powell Co, KY

Eastern Milksnake

RRG, Powell Co, KY

Eastern Black Kingsnake

Stanton, Powell Co, KY

Common Watersnake

Eastern Copperhead

Gray Ratsnake

Common Gartersnake

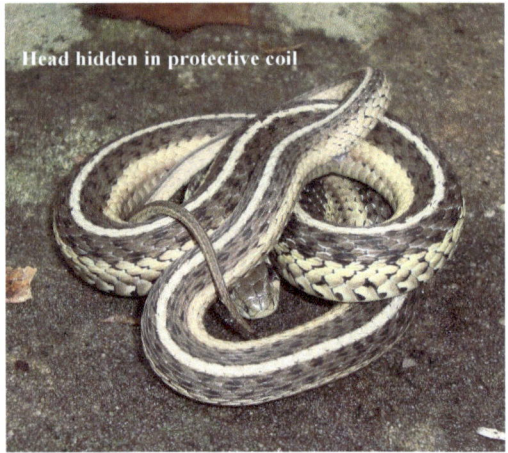

Common Gartersnake, *Thamnophis sirtalis*. (12-36 inches). Gartersnakes are one of the most familiar snakes in the North America, residing in nearly every kind of habitat imaginable including wetlands, open meadows, woodlands, hillsides, ridgetops and are even occasionally found in trees. The Common Gartersnake has one narrow dorsal stripe that runs the entire length of the body, lateral stripes, and a plain, whitish belly. Overall color variable. The diet includes but is not limited to small rodents, frogs, earthworms, leeches, lizards, fish, and even other snakes. Common Gartersnakes almost always bite when handled and are not at all stingy with their foul-smelling musk. It was only recently discovered that Gartersnake saliva contains a mild neurotoxin, produced in the Duvemoy's gland and used to subdue prey. While bites from a Common Gartersnake can cause minor swelling and itching in some humans, prey such as frogs are stunned and immobilized by the neurotoxin, making it easier for the snake to consume. (CP,KN,OB, common, all images from Powell County, KY).

Common Gartersnake

Close up of facial markings

An extraordinary variety of snake coloration patterns have evolved across the globe. While there have been a number of speculations on the function of color and pattern in snakes, the most common theories are camouflage through either background matching and/or disruption of form (Allen et. al 2013). The dorsal stripe of a Common Gartersnake may function as a disruptive pattern or even a decoy (opposite page, figure a). Here's how it might work. When a raccoon comes along and spots a Common Gartersnake in the grass, a chase begins. As the snake crawls away in a zigzagging motion, the dorsal stripe becomes a bewildering target for the raccoon to follow. Why? The dorsal stripe of the snake moves from right to left and back, confusing the raccoon as to which direction the snake is actually going. A split-second delay by the raccoon is all the snake needs to escape. The dorsal stripe may also act as a decoy, keeping the raccoon's attention off the vulnerable head of the snake. This optical illusion suggests that a striped pattern may be more effective in permitting escape than other color patterns such as bands (Lillywhite 2014).

Eastern Black Kingsnake

Adult Eastern Black Kingsnake

Eastern Black Kingsnake, *Lampropeltis nigra.* (36-45 inches). A large bodied species of old fields, rocky hillsides, and open woodlands. Kingsnakes are powerful constrictors—consuming a variety of small mammals, birds, lizards, eggs, and even other snakes including venomous ones such as Rattlesnakes and Copperheads. While juvenile Eastern Black Kingsnakes have bold whitish bands, in adults these bands are only mere traces. Head and facial patterns are examples of outstanding contrast markings (see below). Belly checkered. Kingsnakes rarely bite when handled. (CP,KN,OB, common, RRG, Powell Co, KY).

Eastern Black Kingsnake

Belly patterns strongly developed

Juvenile Eastern Black Kingsnake

Eastern Black Kingsnake

Off with the old and on with the new as an Eastern Black Kingsnake sheds its aged, faded, and worn-out skin for a fresh and glossy one. All snakes shed as they grow, a process that may take place several times a year depending on how well the snake is feeding. (Edmonson County, Kentucky, image by Phil Peak).

Old skin

New skin

Eastern Black Kingsnake

Above an Eastern Black Kingsnake constricting an Eastern Copperhead. Below, a closer look at the head of the Eastern Copperhead under the squeeze. There will be no escape and death will come quickly, at which time the lifeless Copperhead will be swallowed head first. (Trigg County, Kentucky, image by Phil Peak).

Eastern Milksnake

Eastern Milksnake, *Lampropeltis triangulum* (24-36 inches). A medium-sized snake found in a variety of habitats. Belly checkered. Many people still believe that these snakes are capable of milking cows—a ridiculous but interesting anecdote. Eastern Milksnakes are constrictors that seize live prey such as small rodents. Prey is killed by constriction followed by consumption of the prey head first. These snakes will usually bite when handled. (CP,KN,OB, common, all images from Powell Co, KY).

Close-up of facial markings

Eastern Milksnake

Juvenile Eastern Milksnake

Note the checkered belly pattern

Eastern Milksnake

Newly shed Eastern Milksnake

Eastern Milksnake

A healthy Eastern Milksnake

Below image of an Eastern Milksnake in deep shed with notable scale lesions around the eye caused by a fungus called *Ophidiomyces ophiodiicola*. These lesions often develop during hibernation. While many snakes have signs of scale damage in Kentucky, shedding old skin appears to reduce or eliminate these unsightly lesions.

Scarletsnake

Garland County, Arkansas, © Kory G. Roberts

Powell County, KY, John MacGregor

Scarletsnake, *Cemophora coccinea.* (14-20 inches). A small, fossorial, and very secretive species. Similar to Scarlet Kingsnake but bands end on the sides of the Scarletsnake while bands of the Scarlet Kingsnake completely encircle the body, touching on the belly. Although it has been found living in shale banks around Clay City, little is known of the snake's range and habitats within the Red River Basin. Sometimes dug up during building projects or crossing roads on warm summer nights. Diet includes small snakes, lizards, and lizard eggs. Note the shovel-like nose used to burrow underground, see opposite page bottom image. One of Kentucky's most colorful snakes. (KN, rare, Clark Co, KY).

Scarletsnake

Snake in shed, colors are less vivid

Powell County, KY, John MacGregor

Fort Knox area, John MacGregor

Clark County, Will Bird

Note the shovel-like nose

Scarlet Kingsnake (not confirmed from Red River Basin)

Will Bird, Trigg County, Kentucky

Scarlet Kingsnake, *Lampropeltis elapsoides.* (14-20 inches). The Scarlet Kingsnake is most common to the coastal US. In Kentucky, it is known only from western, southeastern, and eastern portions in fragmented locations. While this species can still be found in western portions of the state around LBL, the Scarlet Kingsnake appears to be much less frequent or now absent in eastern Kentucky (no recent sightings exist). However, there are pre-1940 Scarlet Kingsnake records close to Red River Gorge, from Rowan County to the north (less than 30 miles away) and one from Floyd County (around 40 miles) to the southeast (see yellow dots, opposite page). Scarlet Kingsnakes are small fossorial species of mostly pine forests where they are known to winter in old pine stumps. This species resembles the Scarletsnake (confirmed from the Red River Watershed) but differs by having bands that encircle and touch on the belly (bands end at the sides of a Scarletsnake). Their diet consists of lizards, small snakes, baby mice, earthworms, and insects.

Although Scarlet Kingsnakes have not been documented from the Red River Basin, the species might have occurred (or still does) in the past when extensive pine habitat predominated ridgetops of Red River Gorge (RRG); with these habitats mostly disappearing as US Forest Service fire suppression activities increased. Several other examples of southern species tied to pine forests that have lived or are still living in the area include Red-cockaded Woodpeckers (now extirpated from RRG) and the Red Cornsnake, *Pantherophis guttatus,* still extant in RRG, although extremely rare. The last Red-cockaded Woodpecker nest cavity observed in RRG was on the edge of a high sandstone cliff above Red River in the late 1990's (personal observation). Although sparse, small belts of nearly pure pine stands can be found along the edges of the more than 900 miles of sandstone clifflines. These narrow bands of pine bordered by sandstone glades might support Scarlet Kingsnakes but would need to be investigated to prove or disprove the snakes' presence in RRG. (CP, little is known regarding Scarlet Kingsnakes in eastern Kentucky).

Scarlet Kingsnake (not confirmed from Red River Basin)

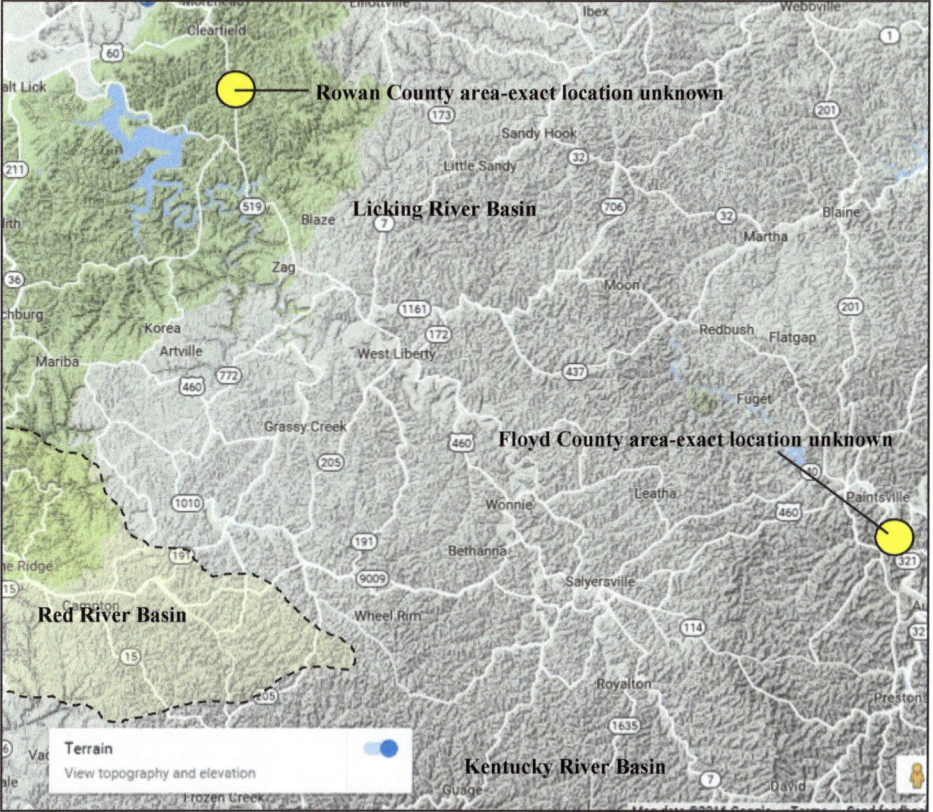

Rowan County area-exact location unknown

Licking River Basin

Floyd County area-exact location unknown

Red River Basin

Kentucky River Basin

Terrain
View topography and elevation

Will Bird, Trigg County, Kentucky

Above a slightly different Scarlet Kingsnake color morph from the same site, not uncommon among many species of snakes.

Gray Ratsnake

Gray Ratsnake, *Pantherophis spiloides.* (42-72 inches, 6 feet). A large-bodied species of old fields, ravines, and open woodlands. Gray Ratsnakes are the longest of the local serpents and are powerful constrictors—consuming a variety small mammals, birds, and a local favorite, chicken eggs. Adults typically with faded pattern on back and belly, not strongly checkered as in Eastern Black Kingsnake. North American Racers have no dorsal pattern except as juveniles. (below image of newly hatching Gray Ratsnakes). This snake will usually bite when handled. (CP,KN,OB, Bowen, Powell Co, KY).

John MacGregor

Gray Ratsnake

Above a baby Gray Ratsnake exhibiting stronger dorsal and belly patterns

Red Cornsnake

Belly of Cornsnake (Mammoth Cave)

Adult

Juvenile

Red Cornsnake, _Pantherophis guttatus._ (30-48 inches). A large species of old fields and open pine woodlands. Red Cornsnakes are powerful constrictors consuming a variety small mammals and birds. Typically with light or dark patterns on back and a whitish, black-checkered belly. This beautiful snake is known from only two populations in Kentucky, one around Mammoth Cave and the other from Red River Gorge. (CP, rare, Red River Gorge, Kentucky).

Red Cornsnake

John MacGregor, Martins Fork, Powell Co, KY

Above close up of a Red Cornsnake caught entering a crayfish burrow, Martins Fork, Red River Gorge and below image of a Red Cornsnake from the Mammoth Cave region which generally have brighter colorations than Red Cornsnakes from Red River Gorge.

Will Bird

Red Cornsnake

First baby Red Cornsnake photographed from RRG, found by Howard Branham (2016)

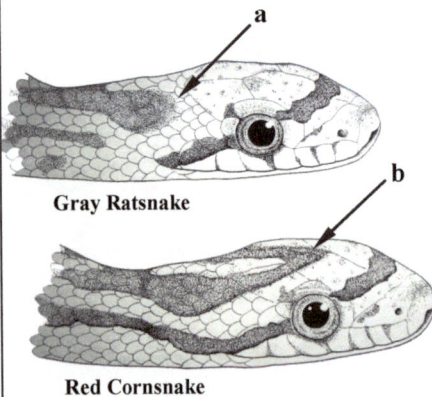

Juvenile heads of Gray Ratsnake and Red Cornsnake compared

Gray Ratsnake

Red Cornsnake

In the Gray Ratsnake, forked bands end at the neck (a). In juvenile Red Cornsnakes, the bands continue and join or nearly join on top of head, just above the eyes (figures b and c)

A juvenile Red Cornsnake (RRG)

131

Red Cornsnake

Adult Red Cornsnake

Will Bird, Powell Co, KY

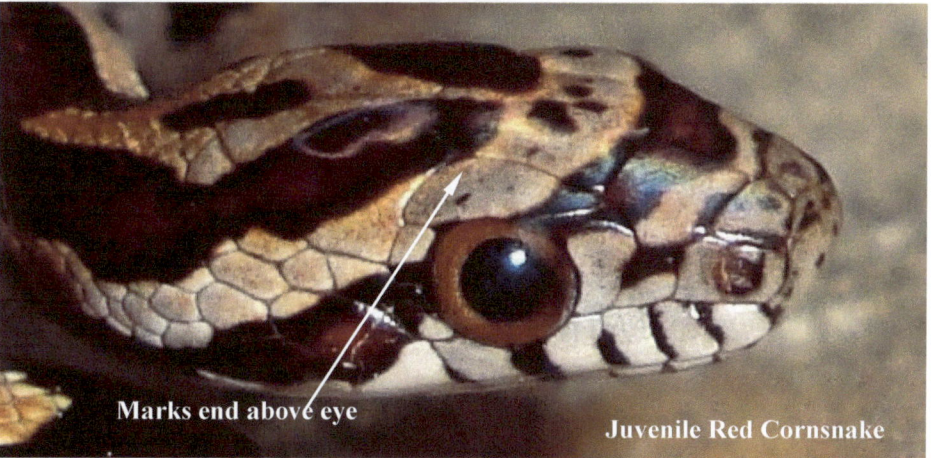

Marks end above eye

Juvenile Red Cornsnake

Powell Co, KY

Marks end here

Juvenile Gray Ratsnake

Powell Co, KY

North American Racer, *Coluber constrictor.* (36-60 inches). A large slender snake of old fields and open woodlands from valley floors to ridgetops and clifflines. North American Racers are alert, fast-moving, quick to flee, and good tree climbers. Adults without any dorsal or belly pattern. The chin is white but the belly is usually dark gray. Juvenile Racers have dark dorsal and belly blotches (page 135). Insects form a major part of the Racer diet, especially for the juveniles and yearlings. This species will almost always bite when handled and one of the few snakes in the state that will occasionally chase a perceived threat. (CP,KN,OB, common, Cane Creek, all images from Powell Co, KY).

Adult North American Racer showing lack of head patterns, white chin, and smooth (non-keeled) glossy scales.

North American Racer (Juvenile)

Juvenile showing head and dorsal patterns

Juvenile showing belly patterns

Adult head

Juvenile head

Rough Greensnake

Rough Greensnake, *Opheodrys aestivus*. (22-32 inches). A small, thin snake of elevated vegetation such as vines, shrubs, and low trees along riparian zones. Bright green, a light, unmarked belly, and purple mouth are the color-themes of this uncommon serpent. Interestingly, the snake turns blue upon death. Eggs are laid in arboreal habitats. Diet includes grasshoppers, crickets, moth larva, and spiders. According to local folklore, bites from this snake can cause uncontrolled laughing fits but the snake rarely bites when handled. (CP,KN,OB, infrequent, all images from RRG area, Powell Co, KY).

Rough Greensnake

Mouth gaping is a defensive behavior

At home in the trees

Common Watersnake

Adult

Common Watersnake, *Nerodia sipedon.* (24-42 inches). An aquatic snake found in any body of water that supplies a diet of fish and frogs. The species has a heavy body and when threatened—like many other snakes—flattens its body and head (opposite page top image). If this fails to deter the threat, the snake will strike repeatedly. This has earned the snake a misguided reputation. In eastern Kentucky, Common Watersnakes continue to be misidentified as Cottonmouths or Water Moccasins, the latter name sometimes applied to any water snake often resulting in the snake's death by the misinformed. This is unfortunate for the Common Watersnake who plays an important role in aquatic ecosystems by consuming sick and dying fish as well as frogs, therefore maintaining balance and health. There is little resemblance between Common Watersnakes and Cottonmouths—especially when comparing their heads (see page 94). Furthermore, contrary to popular belief, a flattened, diamond-shaped head does not mean the snake is venomous. (CP,KN,OB, common, all images from Cane Creek, Powell Co, KY).

Juvenile

Common Watersnake

A flattened, diamond-shaped head does not mean the snake is venomous

Juvenile Common Watersnakes have bolder markings which will fade with age

Queensnake

Queensnake, *Regina septemvittata.* (15-24 inches). A small aquatic snake of creeks littered with flat limestone rocks where the snake's favorite food—newly shed, soft-bodied crayfish—thrive in numbers. Queensnakes rarely bite in self-defense but do not hesitate to squirt foul-smelling fluids from musk glands on any intruder. Queensnakes and Common Watersnakes are found together in Lulbegrud Creek and are easily separated based on the presence or absence of dorsal patterns. Queensnakes are apparently absent from Red River Gorge. (OB, common, Lulbegrud Creek, Clark Co, KY).

Queensnake

Striped belly pattern

Typical habitat, open limestone rock stream, Lulbegrud Creek, Clark Co, KY

Eastern Hog-nosed Snake

Eastern Hog-nosed Snake, *Heterodon platyrhinos.* (20-45 inches). It's been said "**The only good snake is a dead snake**". Evidently the Hog-nosed Snake got the memo! To cheat death, the snake actually fakes its own death by a number of clever strategies to stay alive. The snake's first deception is to spread its neck like a cobra (above image), hissing loudly (which can be quite startling!) giving the snake its local name "blowing viper". If this scare tactic fails to work, smelly anal fluids are released, followed by false strikes with a closed mouth. What happens next is no less amazing. While spitting up bloody-mucus, the "blowing viper" opens its mouth, displays a limp tongue, and rolls over onto its back to complete the deception of death (page 145). While this amazing strategy works well on most predators, unaware humans who "freak out" and usually end up killing the snake—a sad ending to such an animated and spirited animal! Although the Eastern Hog-nosed Snake is capable of delivering bites that become symptomatic in humans (mild swelling and pain), it is not considered medically significant. the diet of the species is almost entirely consists of toads. But toads don't liked being eaten, so in an unconvincing attempt to scare off the snake, the toad will swell up. That is where its fangs (page 145) come into play. As the snake strikes the toad, two things happen. The fangs are used to "pop" the inflated toad, then an amphibian-specific venom is introduced, subduing the toad for consumption. There is a wide range of color variation within local populations (see pages 146-147). (CP,KN,OB, common, all Eastern Hog-nosed Snakes pictured in book are from Estill and Powell Counties, KY).

The Remarkable Eastern Hog-nosed Snake

The head spread

A live Eastern Hog-nosed Snake faking its own death

Fang

The head spread

Eastern Hog-nosed Snake Color Variations from Red River Basin

Eastern Hog-nosed Snake Color Variations from Red River Basin

Mark Gumbert

Eastern Copperhead (venomous)

Eastern Copperhead, *Agkistrodon contortrix.* ((24-36 inches, record 53 inches). Copperheads are medium-sized venomous pit vipers. Although an hourglass pattern is a typical theme, color shades vary considerably, the head usually a copper color. Copperheads can be found just about anywhere from bottomlands to ridgetops, around sandstone or limestone cliffs, under flat rocks in creeks during hot summer months, around pond edges, and even in elevated places such as trees. Diet includes a variety of vertebrate and invertebrate prey. Contrary to popular belief, Copperheads are not antagonistic snakes. People insist that Copperheads are aggressive, confusing a defensive behavior (sitting in place and striking at an intruder) with an aggressive behavior (chasing the intruder and biting). These are very different behaviors. <u>Copperhead venom is mild and there have been no reported fatalities from this species in Kentucky</u>. In fact in the US, there are an estimated 7,000-8,000 bites from venomous snakes annually resulting in less than 5 deaths per year and nearly all from Rattlesnakes. There have been no deaths from Rattlesnake or Copperhead bites in the Gorge, yet every year 1-3 people die from falls, making cliffs—not snakes—the biggest single danger to your life! When a snake is encountered, simply walk around the animal. It will not chase you. Copperheads do not lay eggs but like rattlesnakes have live birth. Baby Copperheads have a greenish-yellow tail used to lure prey within striking distance. Almost certainly one of the most common snakes in Red River Gorge and eastern Kentucky. (CP,KN, common, all images, Powell County, KY).

Eastern Copperhead (venomous)

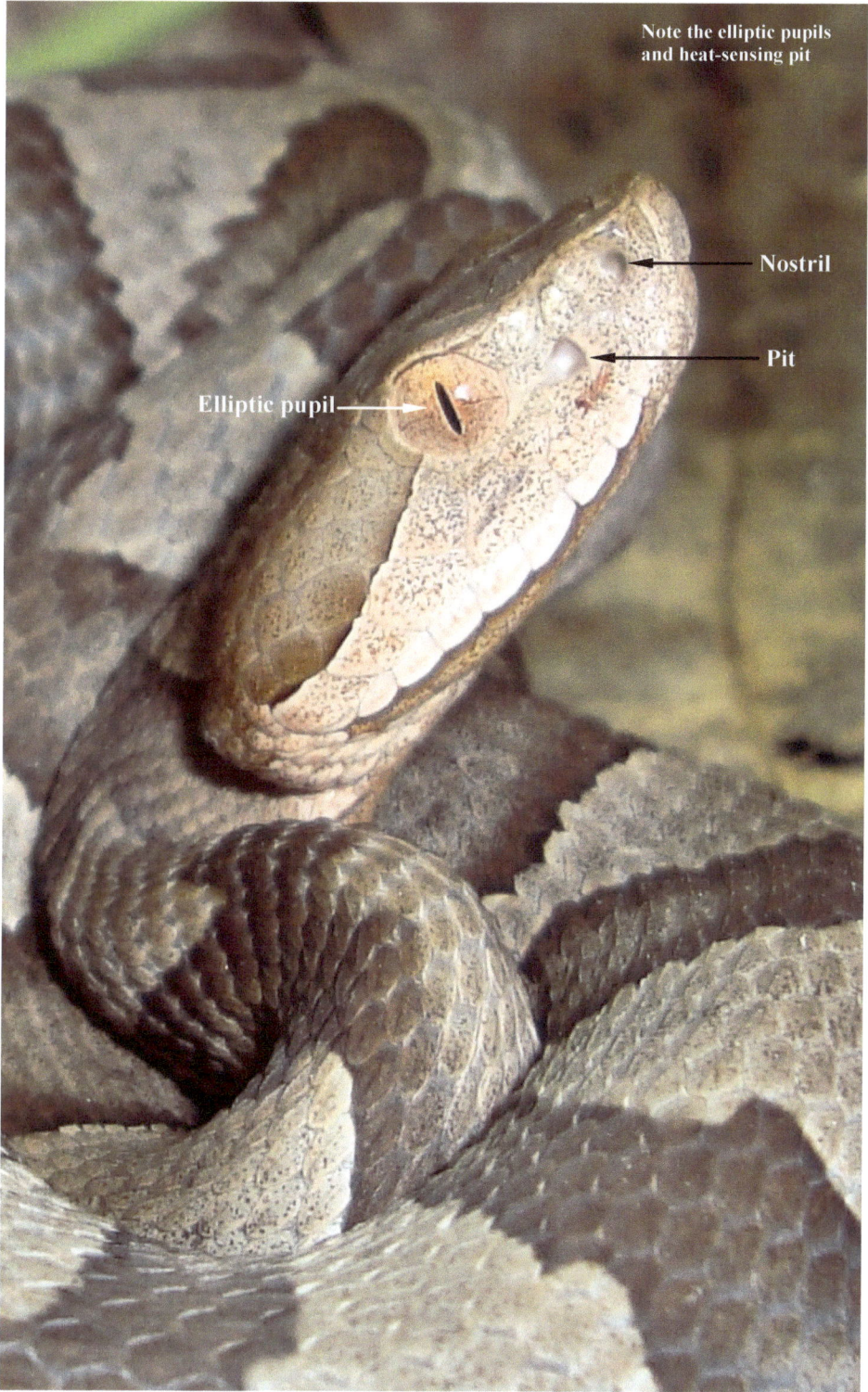

Note the elliptic pupils and heat-sensing pit

Nostril

Pit

Elliptic pupil

Eastern Copperhead, 4 color Variations, all from Powell Co, KY

Eastern Copperhead (venomous)

Note the broken or offset, cross bands

150

Eastern Copperhead Birthing Rock/Den Sites

Birthing site

Mother Copperhead with newborns in the back

Newly shed baby Copperhead with a greenish tail

Birthing Rocks and Dens In springtime, gravid Copperheads and Rattlesnakes emerge from their dens to seek out exposed rocky features (referred to as birthing rocks, above images) where they remain throughout summer. The warm surfaces of the rock help to incubate eggs internally, which by late August early September are born alive. During this 5 to 6 month period, the snakes may not eat or drink as it is a physically demanding time for the mother snakes. After giving live birth to a dozen or so babies, the adults head back to winter dens that may be miles away.

Eastern Copperhead (venomous)

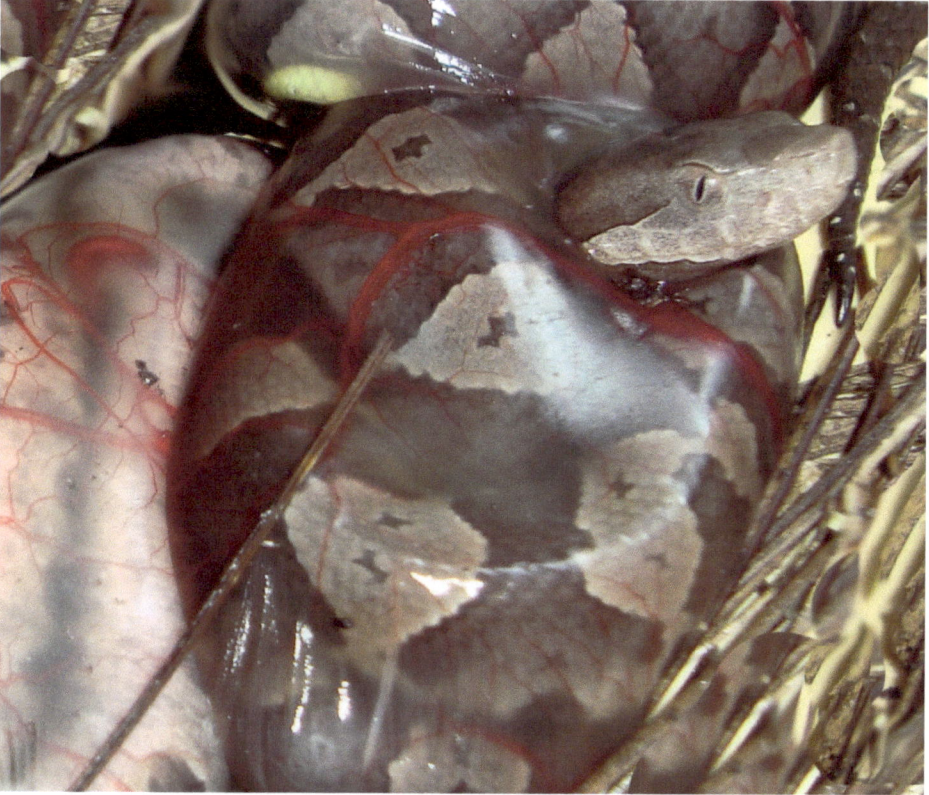

Baby copperheads, like other pit vipers, are born alive but in clear sacks (above image). Within an hour of birth, young copperheads push their way out of the thin, cellophane-like wraps but unlike Timber Rattlesnakes do not stay with their mother long.

Eastern Copperhead (venomous)

Two week old Eastern Copperhead and it's yellow/green-tail

Eastern Copperhead (venomous)

An unusually light color morph of an Eastern Copperhead hunting Green Frogs in a pond on Gritter Ridge, Powell County, Kentucky.

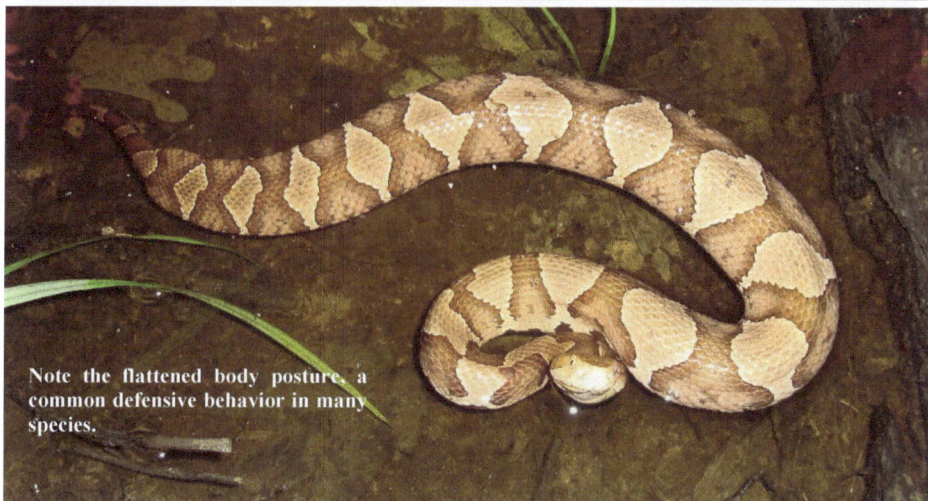

Note the flattened body posture, a common defensive behavior in many species.

154

Copperhead Ecology/Research in the Red River Gorge

By Stephen Richter, Jocelyn Hendricks, Jesse Sockman, and Henderson Gull
Division of Natural Areas and Department of Biological Sciences
Eastern Kentucky University

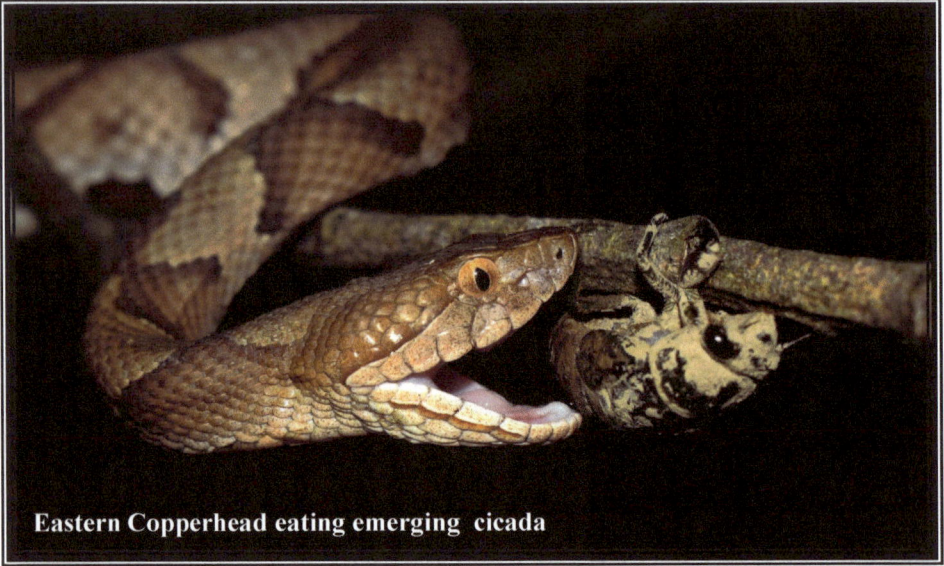

Eastern Copperhead eating emerging cicada

Images by Sarah Phillips, *Capturing Contortrix*

The Red River Gorge of the Daniel Boone National Forest provides a multitude of recreational opportunities to the public while also providing important habitat to native flora and fauna. Therefore, the need to balance public engagement, economic viability, and preservation of natural resources becomes incredibly important. Natural recreational areas facilitate human-wildlife interactions, which can result in negative consequences for both humans and wildlife. This is especially true for animals that humans perceive as dangerous. Since 2015, a collaborative group of field biologists have been studying Eastern Copperheads, *Agkistrodon contortrix*, in the Gorge to reduce conflict, some perceived and some actual, between these snakes and humans. The study system was established by personnel from the National Park Service, U.S. Forest Service, Kentucky Department of Fish and Wildlife Resources, and the Louisville Zoo before Eastern Kentucky University took the lead. Research continues to be collaborative and is driven primarily by undergraduate and graduate students in the lab of Dr. Stephen Richter.

By studying copperhead life history, we can understand variation in the activity and behaviors of individuals, patterns of distribution, local abundances, and how these relate to environmental cues across years. This is important from a scientific perspective, but more importantly, we can use this knowledge to predict the intersection of copperhead ecology with human use of the land. Another valuable aspect of this system is that through our daily monitoring, we create a platform for education and awareness that lowers perceived risk, lowers actual risk of bites, and continues to provide data-driven, sustainable management recommendations to the US Forest Service that benefit both snakes and recreational site users.

Our work thus far has primarily focused on one specific aspect of copperhead ecology that brings humans and copperheads to the same area. During the summer months, copperheads search for annual cicadas to consume as the nymphs emerge from the ground and climb trees to molt into adults. This predictable food source of nymphs and adults is important to many species, including flying squirrels, birds, and bats. Just as feeding on cicadas is not unique to copperheads, their feeding on cicadas is not unique to the Gorge. This phenomenon has not only been observed in other parts of the Daniel Boone National Forest, in Big South Fork National Recreational Area, and in homeowners' yards in Kentucky, but reports have been made for private and public lands across the eastern US. Even though this phenomenon is not unique to the Gorge, it is critical to understand the local ecology of copperheads and to educate climbers, hikers, and campers about the importance of these snakes and why open rockfaces and other open habitats are essential to their life history. The end goal is to continue maintaining habitats in the Gorge for copperheads and human use while reducing potentially negative outcomes for each. To keep up with our research, follow along at https://richterlab.weebly.com/copperheads.html.

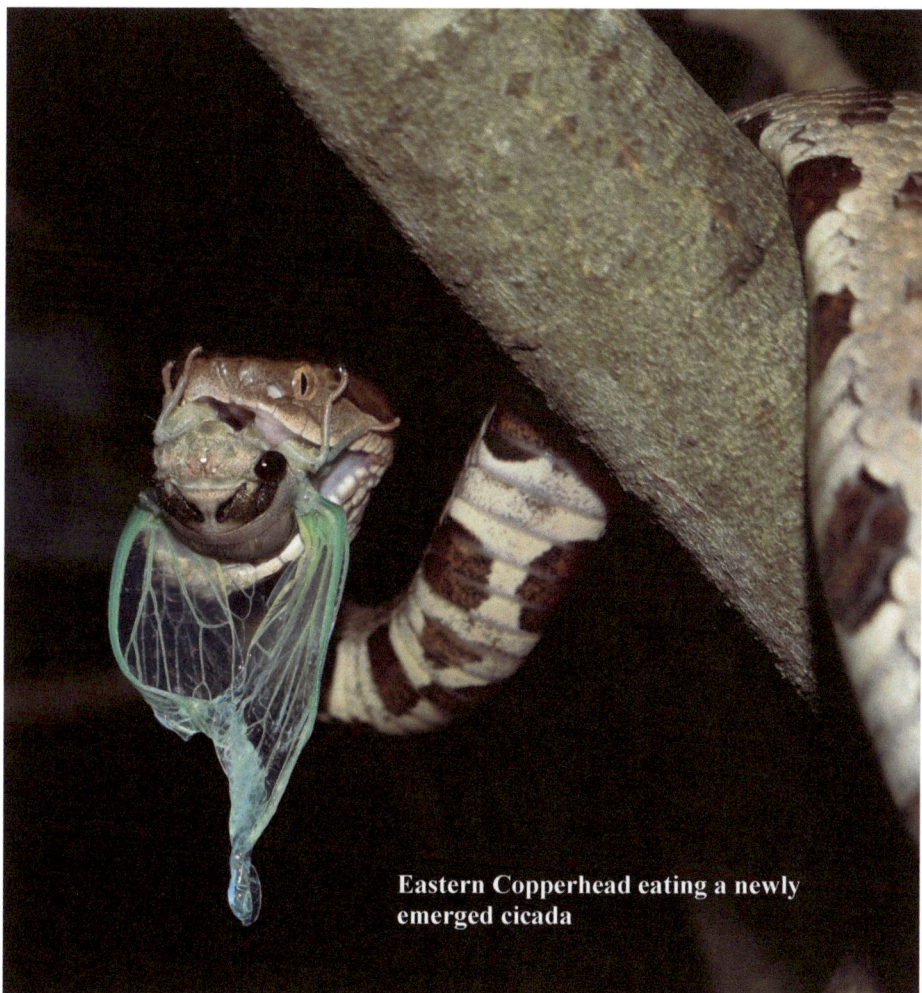

Eastern Copperhead eating a newly emerged cicada

Images by Sarah Phillips, *Capturing Contortrix*

Eastern Copperhead Feeding

Eastern Copperhead climbing tree to feed on newly morphed cicada

Eastern Copperhead eyeing cicada meal

Eastern Copperhead Feeding

Eastern Copperhead eating a newly emerging cicada

Timber Rattlesnake (venomous)

Timber Rattlesnake, *Crotalus horridus.* (36-60 inches, record 74 inches or 6 feet). The Timber Rattlesnake is a large heavy-bodied, venomous pit viper. Located between the nostril and eye is a highly evolved radiant-heat sensing organ called a pit used to track warm-blooded animals (see page 96). The pit allows the snake to form a thermal profile of its prey even in total darkness from several feet away. Timber Rattlesnakes are a variable species in terms of color, ranging from nearly all black to bright yellow. This color variability has led to the mistaken and local belief that multiple species of rattlesnakes occur in eastern Kentucky. While Copperheads are found throughout the entire Red River Basin, Timber Rattlesnakes are limited to small, isolated pockets, remaining somewhat of a mystery. Diet includes a variety of small mammals, Eastern Chipmunks being a favorite food. Rattlesnake venom is strong enough to kill humans but with proper treatment—rarely fatal. <u>All reported rattlesnake deaths in Kentucky have been in people that were bitten during snake-handling church services and who have refused proper medical treatment</u>. Like Copperheads, Rattlesnakes do not lay eggs but have live birth. In Kentucky, young Timber Rattlesnakes remain near their mothers for a week or more after birth and will quickly crawl over to her when threatened. No other Kentucky snake demonstrates any kind of parental care. There is recent literature showing young Timber Rattlesnakes following mom to the hibernacula, but this is yet to be observed in the state. No large communal dens have been documented in Kentucky and most, if not all, of Kentucky's Rattlesnakes hibernate as singles or in very small groups. (CP,KN, infrequent, Powel Co, KY).

159

Timber Rattlesnake (venomous)

Nothing more than loose-fitting sections of dead skin, the rattle is a wonder of evolution. Every time a snake sheds—often several times a year depending on how well the snake is eating—a new segment or button is added to the rattle. This negates the belief that the age of a rattlesnake can be determined by the number of buttons. Two widely-accepted theories for the evolution of the rattle are: 1) the rattle serves as a warning of the snake's presence and 2) the rattle is used as a startle-mechanism—stopping potential prey in its tracks—giving the snake ample time to thermally locate and strike. Many other species of snakes also vibrate their tails when feeling threatened.

Above the fangs of a rattlesnake with a double set on the right side. This is not unusual since strikes at prey or in defense can damage these structures and therefore, need to be constantly replaced throughout the snake's lifetime. This ensures that the snake always has a set of sharp piercing fangs to deliver its venom.

Timber Rattlesnake (venomous)

This female Timber Rattlesnake just gave live birth to eight (still wet from birth) babies and four unfertile eggs (figure a showing one of the four) that never developed inside the mother. This is not uncommon. Clutch sizes can vary from 5 to 20 young depending on the size and age of the female rattlesnake. Powell County, KY.

Timber Rattlesnake (venomous)

Above newborn Timber Rattlesnakes remain near their mother for a week or more after birth and will quickly crawl to her when threatened. No other Kentucky snake exhibits this kind of parental care! Note the lackluster skin and opaque eyes of the week-old rattlesnakes nearing their first skin shedding. After shedding, skin colors are more vibrant (see next page). Below the tail of a newborn Timber Rattlesnake with a single button; each shed will add a new button. Images from Powell County, KY.

Baby Timber Rattlesnake (venomous)

Above images of an unusually marked baby Timber Rattlesnake; note the solid dark -dorsal band which is typically broken in most individuals (see page 165).

Baby Timber Rattlesnake (venomous)

Above a common Timber Rattlesnake color morph found in Red River Gorge. A snake often confused with the Timber Rattlesnake is the Eastern Hog-nosed Snake (below image). While at first glance it may appear similar, the Eastern Hog-nosed Snake has a slightly upturned nose, round pupils (rattlesnakes have elliptical pupils) and lacks a rattle. Color highly variable in both species of snakes.

Eastern Hog-nosed Snake

A gray color morph with a pale yellow dorsal band running down its back and a dark head from Chop Chestnut, Powell Co, KY.

Timber Rattlesnake (striking color morphs from Powell Co, KY)

A yellow color morph with a darkened tail, Natural Bridge State Park, Powell Co, KY, image by John MacGregor.

.

Warning Signs of an Agitated Snake!

Snakes use a variety of scare-tactics when threatened including flattening the body, neck, and head, mouth-gaping, false strikes, and tail vibrating. Below a Gray Ratsnake is seen exhibiting one of these effective tactics. If these strategies fail to work, actual full-on contact bites will usually follow, so pay close attention to these warning signs! Research has shown that most people bitten by wild snakes have engaged in catching, harassing, or killing the serpent.

John MacGregor, Fulton County, KY

Author receiving a proper and well-deserved bite from an Eastern Milksnake

167

A male Eastern Fence Lizard in full breeding colors, RRG

Lizards

Occasionally mistaken for salamanders which are amphibians, lizards are reptiles that have dry, scaly skin, sharp claws at the ends of each toe, and are often seen basking in the sun. Lizards are also speedy on their feet. In contrast, salamanders have moist skin, no scales, or claws, live under moist cover, and in general, are slower moving, although some salamanders can disappear from sight rather quickly. Many locals fish with "Spring-lizards", which are usually Dusky Salamanders.

Lizards are largely diurnal (active during the day) and more commonly observed on dry ridgetops—especially during the hotter summer months—while salamanders are nocturnal (active during the night) and more easily found below the clifflines around streams and on moist hillsides. But there are always exceptions to this rule. During the springtime, ridgetop ponds are full of Spotted and Jefferson Salamanders that quickly disappear into deep burrows after mating and egg-laying while Eastern Newts remain in the ponds all summer long.

Five lizard species are reported from the Red River Basin and although relatively common (except for the Coal Skink), these masters of disguise are rarely seen by the casual observer, blending in well with their surroundings. But they are seldom far from a good sunny spot to heat up their ectothermic bodies. Lizards feed on a variety of invertebrates including grasshoppers, crickets, and spiders. Eggs are usually laid under or in debris such as rotting logs in advanced stages of decay or under rocks.

Broad-headed Skink

Male Broad-headed Skink

Broad-headed Skink, *Plestiodon laticeps.* (6-12 inches). A large, thick bodied skink of rather dry sites such as open sandstone ridgetops. Eggs are laid under logs and other debris and guarded by females until hatching. The Broad-headed Skink usually has 5 upper labials in front of the eye on each side of the head, and the Common Five-lined Skink usually has 4 on each side. This works about 85% of the time for ID. Some have 4 on one side and 5 on the other. The Broad-headed Skink usually has one enlarged postlabial or none bordering the ear opening; the Common Five-lined Skink usually has a pair of postlabials there (see opposite page). (CP,KN,OB, common, top image from Carlisle Co. KY and bottom image from Gritter Ridge, Powell Co. KY).

A gravid female Broad-headed Skink

Skink Heads Compared

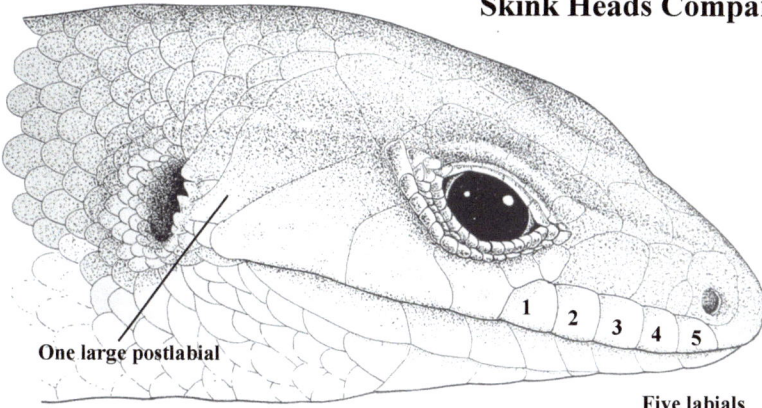

One large postlabial

Broad-headed Skink

1 2 3 4 5

Five labials

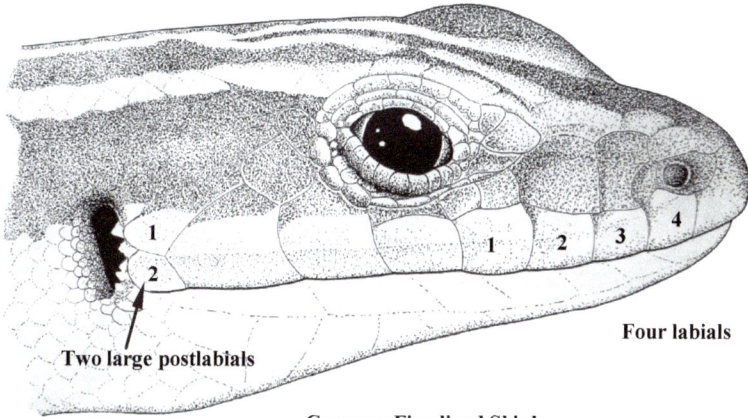

Two large postlabials

Common Five-lined Skink

1 2

1 2 3 4

Four labials

Common Five-lined Skinks courting, male on top, Rowan County, Kentucky

Steve Bonney

Common Five-lined Skink

Juvenile Common Five-lined Skink

Common Five-lined Skink, *Plestiodon fasciatus.* (5-8 inches). A medium-sized skink of open habitats such as cliff edges, large dead trees, and rock piles. An excellent climber, the Common Five-lined Skink will not hesitate to escape over a cliff edge. Like all lizards, it enjoys basking in sunny places. Easily confused with the Broad-headed Skink, the Common Five-lined Skink has 4 labials and has 2 large postlabials (see page 170). There is a local myth that the "blue tails" of Common Five-lined Skinks are poisonous to cats that eat them. Although conspicuous colors can and do advertise noxious traits, some animals use bold colors simply as a bluff or a decoy, drawing attention away from vulnerable areas like the head. After eating a skink, some veterinarians diagnose cats exhibiting illness with a condition called feline vestibular syndrome. The Merck Veterinary Manual suggests that a parasitic fluke *Platynosomum concinnum* which affects a number of organisms including lizards may be affecting cats that eat an infected lizard. Nevertheless, the scientific evidence for these claims remains unsettled. (CP,KN,OB, common, all images from RRG, Powell Co, KY).

171

Common Five-lined Skink

The bright blue color of a juvenile's tail fades as the lizard matures

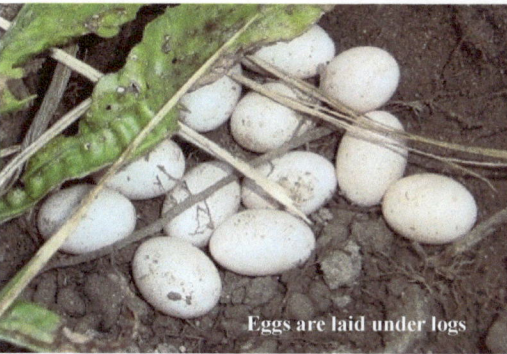

Eggs are laid under logs

Note the long toes

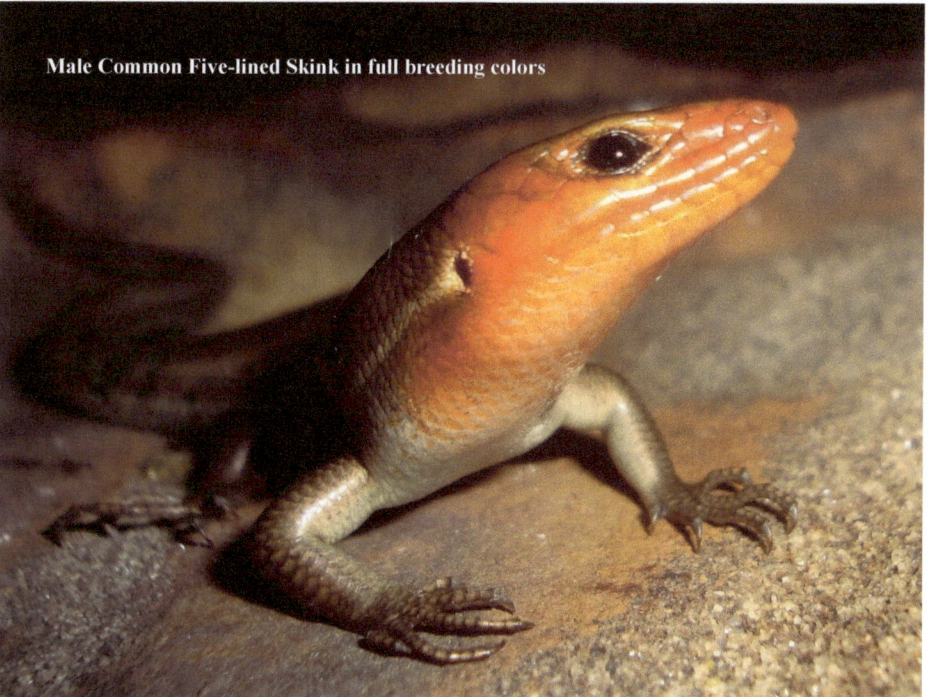

Male Common Five-lined Skink in full breeding colors

Coal Skink

Dark lateral line wide and border by bold white stripes

Little Brown Skink

a

Ear opening

Coal Skink

b

Ear opening

Coal Skink, *Plestiodon anthracinus.* (5-7 inches). In the Red River Watershed, the Coal Skink has been found on Furnace Mountain and mixed woodlands on sandstone ridge tops. Coal Skinks are active by day—consuming a variety of invertebrates. The best field character in separating a Coal Skink and a Little Brown Skink is the lateral stripe that passes over the ear opening in the Little Brown Skink (a) but passes through the ear opening in the Coal Skink (b). (CP, rare, photos taken 6/26/2021, Gritter Ridge, Powell County, KY).

Little Brown Skink

Little Brown Skink, *Scincella lateralis.* (3-5 inches). A small ground-dwelling skink that hunts a variety of leaf-litter insects. Like the Coal Skink, if water is nearby, it to will dive in—staying submerged or use any nearby cover for refuge until danger passes. Similar to Coal Skink but generally about half its size and the lateral stripe passes over the ear opening (in Coal Skinks, the lateral stripe crosses the ear opening, see opposite page). (CP,KN,OB, common, all images from Cane Creek, Powell Co, KY).

Eastern Fence Lizard

Male Fence Lizard in full breeding colors

Eastern Fence Lizard, *Sceloporus undulatus.* (4-7 inches). A lizard of sunny sandstone outcrops, the Eastern Fence Lizard will escape predators up trees or undersides of logs. Male Eastern Fence Lizards are strikingly beautiful during mating season. Eastern Fence Lizards eat a variety of invertebrates. A yet-to-be-identified protein found by UC Berkeley entomologists in the blood of Western Fence Lizards has been shown to kill Lyme disease bacteria in ticks that feed on the lizards, hence Lyme disease remains rare in California. It is not known if Eastern Fence Lizard blood carries any natural immunity properties similar to that of the Western Fence Lizard. Eastern Fence Lizards bury their eggs in loose sandy soil. (CP,KN,OB, common, Cane Creek, Powell Co, KY).

A Fence Lizard playing dead

Male in breeding colors

175

Eastern Fence Lizard

A female Eastern Fence Lizard

Scales

Claws

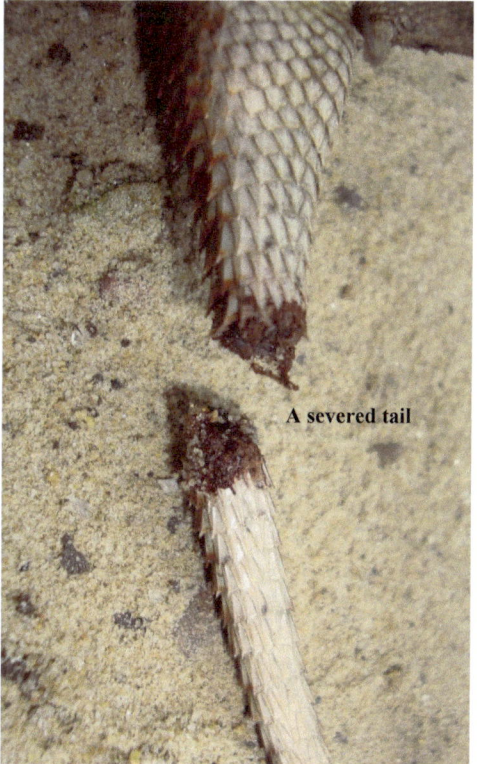

A severed tail

Above the severed tail of an Eastern Fence Lizard. Skinks and lizards are capable of caudal autonomy and tail regeneration. If toes or tail segments are lost from predator attacks or some other injury, they can regenerate these parts, although not as fully formed as the original ones.

The Mysterious Turkey-Turtle (Fact or Fiction?)

Local legends and folklore occur everywhere, and the Red River Gorge is no exception! We stumbled upon this peculiar looking animal while doing research for the book in the yard of local resident, Randle Rogers. Part snapping turtle, part turkey, this "jack-a-lope" of the Red River Gorge defies reason or does it?

While the turkey turtle is just the result of a creative mind, fact is often stranger than fiction. Take for example the Hoatzin Bird of South America. We know that birds are distantly related to reptiles. Genetic research has shown that the Hoatzin may be more lizard than bird. The Hoatzin is the last surviving member of an Avian lineage that branched off in its own direction 64 million years ago, shortly after the extinction event that killed the non-avian dinosaurs. The Hoatzin seen as living evidence of the transition between reptiles and birds, the wing claws of young Hoatzin birds frequently cited as proof of an ancient ancestry.

The hard shells of turtles are another example of a stranger than fiction sensation. Shells are marvels of evolution unlike anything else found in nature. Think all turtles have hard shells? Think again! The Spiny Softshell turtle has a shell that is more like a piece of leather than a shell. Read on to learn more about the fascinating turtles of the Red River Gorge.

Turtles

Eight species of turtles are reported from the Red River Basin or in the Kentucky River near the confluence of the Red River. While seven species are decisively aquatic, one species—the Eastern Box Turtle—is entirely terrestrial. Turtles are reptiles having ancestors dating back some 220 million years. The largest turtle to have ever lived was *Archelon ischyros*, a late Cretaceous sea turtle the size of an SUV. The largest living turtle today is the leatherback sea turtle which reaches a length of six and half feet and weighs in at around 2000 pounds. But turtles of the Red River Basin are considerably smaller, the largest species—the Snapping Turtle—having a shell length of around 15 inches (record 19 inches) and a weight of 10-35 pounds (record 75 pounds). In contrast, the smallest turtle is the Eastern Musk Turtle at only four inches long.

The turtle shell is a wonder of evolution unlike anything else on planet Earth. First and foremost, the shell completely encloses the vital organs of the turtle, and in some cases, the turtle's head. For the terrestrial Eastern Box Turtle, the shell is a mobile home and a nearly impenetrable fortress, allowing the turtle to safely park just about anywhere it wants. Aquatic turtles, however, cannot fully close their shells, so finding a shelter like a hole in the bank or patch of thick vegetation is critical to their survival. Turtles eat a variety of food from vegetation, carrion, invertebrates, and fish. Turtle eggs are always laid in terrestrial habitats. Even aquatic turtles will leave their watery homes and travel great distances to lay their eggs in sandy or other loose soils where primary incubation takes place.

Eastern Box Turtle

Eastern Box Turtle, *Terrapene carolina.* (4-7 inches). The Eastern Box Turtle carries one of the most colorfully patterned carapaces of any North American turtle. Although the species is entirely terrestrial, during the hot summer months of July and August, Eastern Box Turtles are often in and around mud holes and pond edges cooling down and can even swim when the need arises. Eastern Box turtles are the only turtle of 8 species found in the Red River Basin that can completely close its shell, protecting all its soft body parts. A tight-fitting shell has its advantages if you live on land with hungry predators—discouraging even the most persistent critters like raccoons. Box Turtles are omnivorous, eating a variety of foods including fruits, berries, grasses, mushrooms, carrion and even salamanders (opposite page). While Snapping Turtle flesh is considered a delicacy by many, the meat of the Eastern Box Turtle can be highly toxic—even fatal—a result of the turtle's appetite for poisonous mushrooms. This may explain the bright "warning" colors of the shell. One way to distinguish the sex of the Box Turtle is by examining the back portion of the plastron. In males, there is a built-in depression (figure a, right image), which helps keep male turtles in position on females during copulation. Males also have bright red eyes. One of the longest living animals in North America, wild Eastern Box Turtles can live for more than 100 years. These are the most common turtles kept as pets worldwide with the pet trade contributing to greatly reduced numbers in the eastern United States. In Kentucky, it is illegal to buy or sell Eastern Box Turtles unless you first apply for and receive a wildlife propagation permit. (CP,KN,OB, common, Cane Creek, Powell Co, KY).

179

Eastern Box Turtle

A female Eastern Box Turtle burying 4 newly laid eggs in sand, Gritter Ridge, Powell Co, KY

Eastern Box Turtle eating a Northern Red Salamander, Powell County Kentucky

180

The color patterns on the carapace and head of Eastern Box Turtles are as individual as a human fingerprint. Pictured above are six different Eastern Box Turtle shells, illustrating a wide variation. (All shells pictured from Powell County, Kentucky).

Eastern Box Turtle

Shell of hatchling Eastern Box Turtle, colors intensify with age, Gritter Ridge, Powell Co, KY

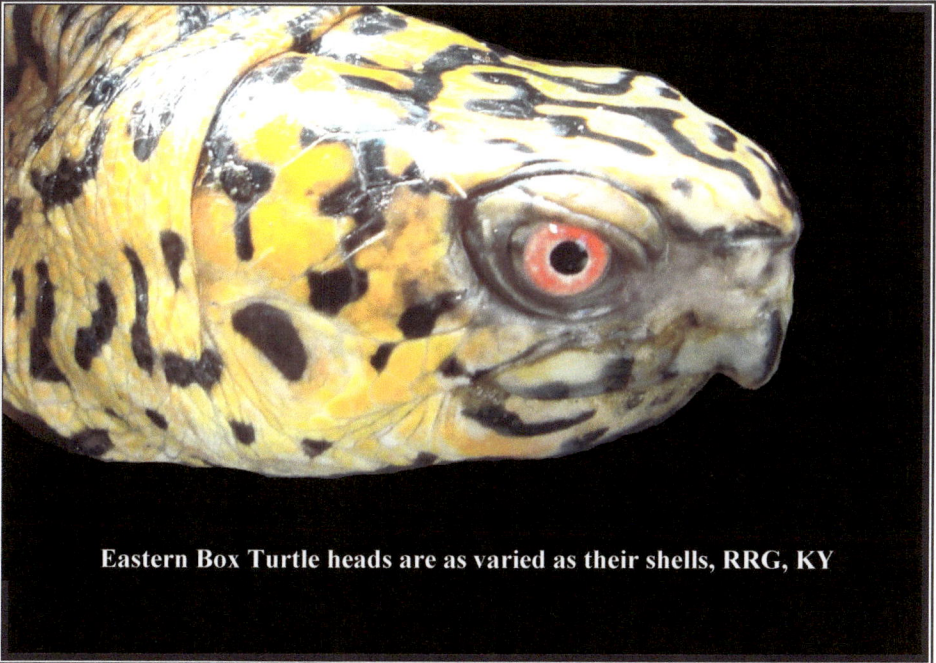

Eastern Box Turtle heads are as varied as their shells, RRG, KY

Snapping Turtle

Snapping Turtle, *Chelydra serpentina*. (8-19 inches). Looking more like a rotting log than an animal, the Snapping Turtle is an astonishing example of flawless evolution. Changing little in more than 90 million years, this prehistoric reptile swam with the dinosaurs, surviving several mass extinction events. The species can live practically anywhere there is standing water, rivers, creeks, ponds, oxbows, and even drainage ditches. No doubt nearly every pond within the Red River Basin has at least one resident Snapping Turtle. When conditions become over-crowded, surplus turtles move—wandering for miles through thick brush, dry ridgetops, and even high mountaintops to find a new home. Eating everything from carrion to vegetation, Snapping Turtles are never far from a palatable food source. It is a widely believed myth that Snapping Turtles in a fishpond will decimate the fish population. But nothing could be further from the truth. Having these ancient animals in a pond will only improve the quality by culling out sick and dying fish. While they occasionally take healthy fish and young ducks, the overall benefits of their presence far outweigh the negative aspects. Snapping Turtles are the vultures of aquatic ecosystems and for this reason have enormous value in such environments. (CP,KN,OB, common, RRG, Powell Co, KY).

Bony scutes on tail

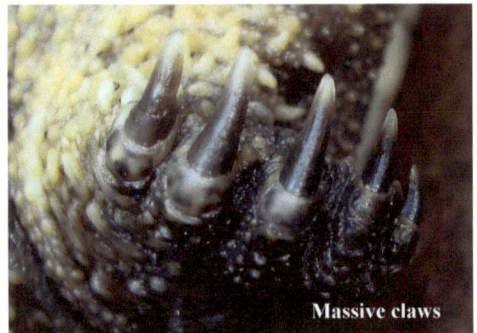

Massive claws

Snapping Turtle

Barbels are thought to be used as a sensory organ

Note the bony scutes on the tail and rough, serrated shell, RRG Powell Co, KY

Eastern Spiny Softshell

Note the vague outline of bony structures comprising the spine and ribs

Eastern Spiny Softshell, *Apalone spiniferus.* (5-17 inches). Softshell turtles are unusual in that they have pliable (not rigid) shells, devoid of the usual scales and scutes seen in other turtle species. Living mostly in rivers, larger streams, and occasionally in lakes, the Eastern Spiny Softshell consumes a variety of fish, crayfish, and aquatic invertebrates. Interestingly, males have tiny projections covering the entire carapace, making the shell feel like coarse sandpaper. The species may be seen floating on the surface but more often covered in mud or sand with only the head protruding where the long, telescoping neck and snorkel-like snout are utilized to the fullest extent. This strategy allows the turtle to remain inconspicuous right under the nose of a nearby human or potential predator. (CP,KN,OB, common, Natural Bridge State Park, Powell Co, KY).

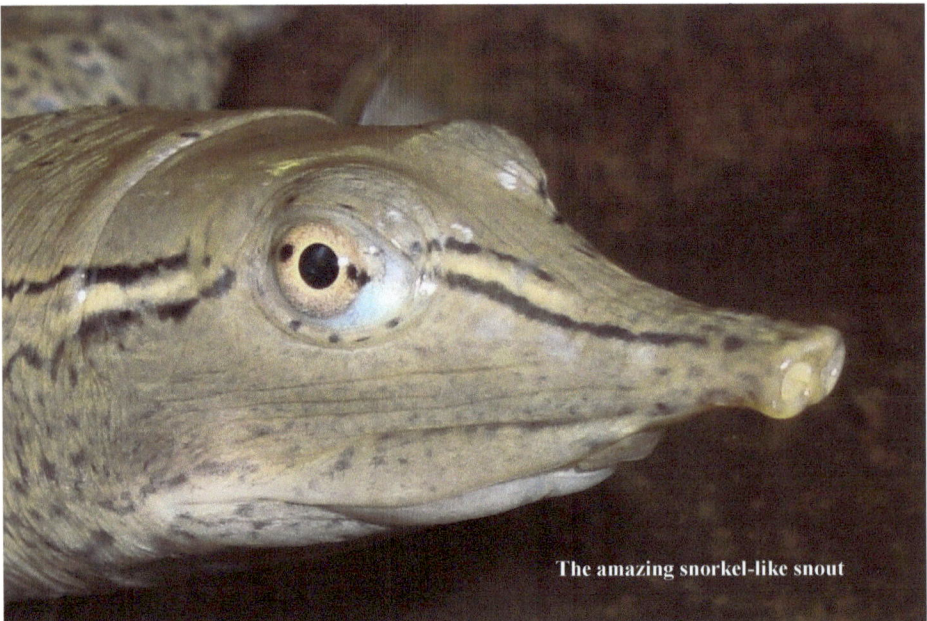

The amazing snorkel-like snout

185

Eastern Spiny Softshell

Foot and claws

The snorkel-like snout

Long telescoping neck

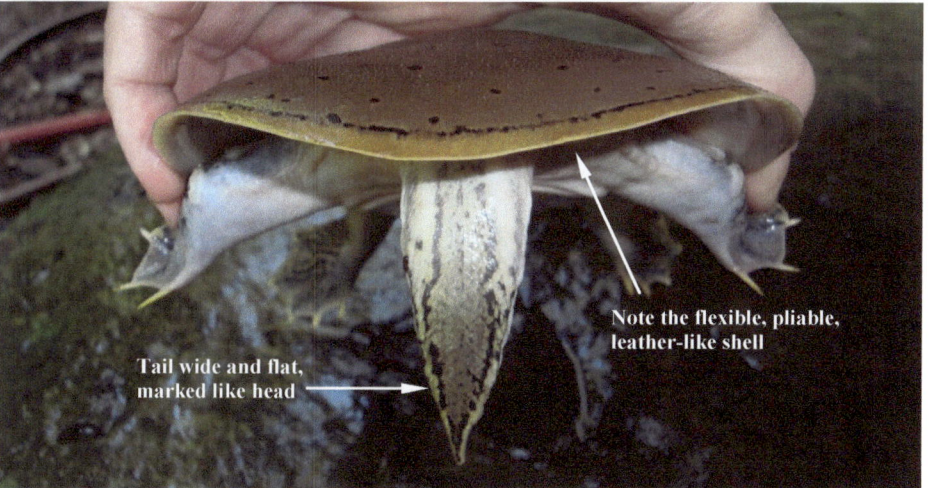
Note the flexible, pliable, leather-like shell

Tail wide and flat, marked like head

Eastern Musk Turtle

Eastern Musk Turtle, *Sternotherus odoratus.* (2-5 inches). Eastern Musk Turtles are not famous for their good looks or lavish taste in a diverse cuisine of snails, clams, crayfish, tadpoles, fish, and carrion but for their resolute and memorable stench! Musk Turtles are the skunks of the turtle world, containing two glandular openings located on each side of the body from which smelly secretions are expelled. When harassed, the turtle releases its load upon the trespasser that can smell worse than a week-old, roadkill possum. Musk Turtles are also good tree climbers, ascending as high as 6 feet or more to bask in the sun. Although the species can be quite abundant in some habitats, this secretive little turtle is rarely observed in the wild. Baby Musk Turtles are cute as a button and not much bigger. But don't be fooled, all turtles will bite in self-defense if given the opportunity. (CP,KN,OB, common, Stanton, Powell Co, KY).

Eastern Musk Turtle

Barbel

The stubby tail

Foot and claws

Painted Turtle

Painted Turtle, *Chrysemys picta* (4-7 inches). Painted Turtles are exactly what the name implies, colorful! They are generally abundant where they occur. In the Red River Basin, Painted Turtles are most common around Clay City and "Beaver Pond", Stanton's original name, where the Red River carved out the widest floodplain in the watershed. Before early settlement by Europeans, this broad valley had countless beaver dams which created immense wetlands—perfect habitat for aquatic turtles. These dams however were drained to grow crops, and today all that remains are just a few scattered wetlands. Nevertheless, Painted Turtles have survived and can still be found with little effort. Their diet includes invertebrates, aquatic snails, young mussels, and fish. The best way to observe these colorful turtles is to look for them basking on floating logs of ponds with the help of a pair of binoculars. (CP,KN,OB, common, Stanton, Powell Co, KY).

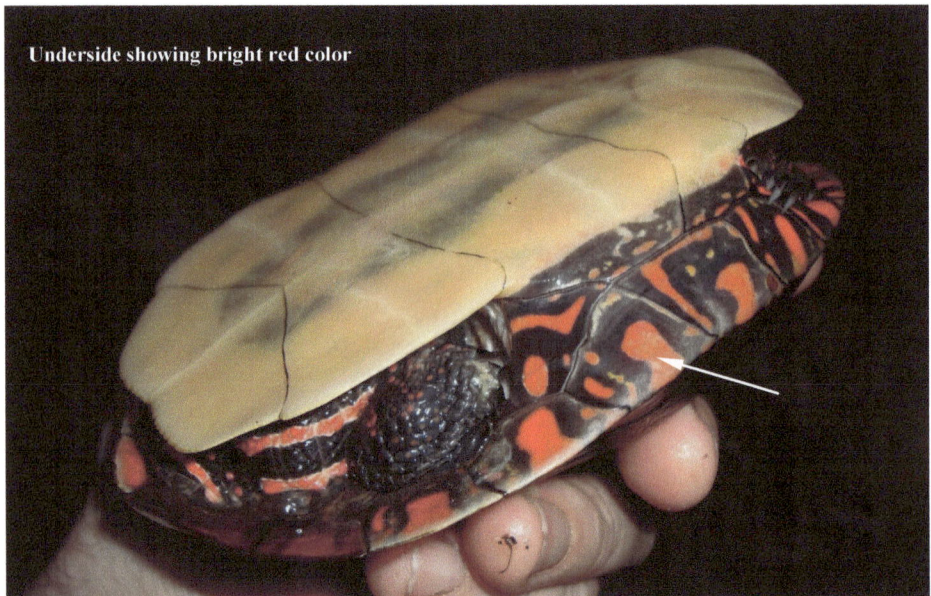

Underside showing bright red color

Painted Turtle

Eyes are striped

The long claws of a male

Pond Slider

Pond Slider, *Trachemys scripta.* (5-11 inches). Similar to Map and Painted Turtles, the Pond Slider differs by having a broad reddish stripe behind the eye (not yellow as in Map and Painted); the red stripe being a unique trait among North American turtles. This is a species of still waters with muddy bottoms and ample vegetation to hide. Like Painted and Map turtles, Pond Sliders also bask in the sun on logs and floating debris. Aquatic snails and crayfish are the primary food sources for the species. Like Map turtles, Pond Sliders are difficult to observe in the wild but float trips down lower portions of the Red River should yield some sightings. (CP,KN,OB, common, Kentucky Reptile Zoo, Slade, Kentucky).

Northern Map Turtle

Northern Map Turtle, *Graptemys geographica.* (3-10 inches). Similar to the Painted Turtle, but lacking the bright red color of the underside of carapace. The Pond Slider has a red spot behind the eye (not yellow as in Map Turtle). In addition, Map Turtles have faint map-like markings on the carapace. Map Turtles are typically found in rivers which make it more difficult to observe than Painted Turtles (a pond species). Males and juveniles eat mostly insects while adult females eat clams and snails, hence the massive jaws. Although unable to close its shell like the Eastern Box Turtle, the Northern Map Turtle can fully retract its head, disappearing in a heap of protective skin (see below). (CP,KN,OB, common, all Red River Boat Dock, Red and Kentucky River confluence, Clark Co, KY).

Northern Map Turtle

Plastron (bottom of shell)

Carapace (top of shell)

Adult Map Turtle

Hatchling Map Turtle

Ouachita Map Turtle

Will Bird

Ouachita Map Turtle, *Graptemys ouachitensis.* (5-11 inches). Similar to the Northern Map Turtle but differs by having small roundish spots under chin and eye (the Northern Map Turtle has stripes under chin and under eye). Both the Pond Slider and Painted Turtles are without the spots under the chin and eye. A species of still waters with muddy bottoms and ample vegetation to hide, this species is most often observed basking in the sun on logs. Aquatic snails and crayfish are the primary food sources. <u>Ouachita Map Turtles have been observed in the Kentucky River in Estill County (pers. comm. John MacGregor, 20016), so are expected to occur in lower portions of the Red River.</u> (OB, Kentucky River, Estill Co, KY).

John MacGregor, Kentucky River, Estill Co, KY

Ouachita Map Turtle

John MacGregor, Kentucky River, Estill Co, KY

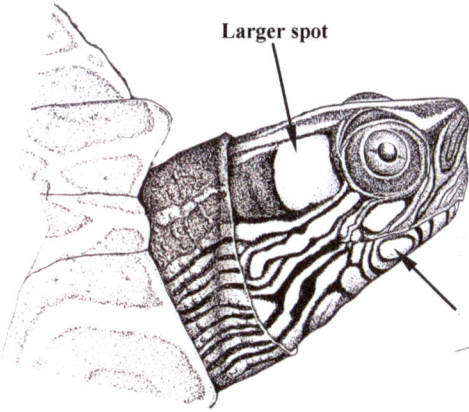

Ouachita Map Turtle

Larger spot

Ouachita Map Turtle, *Graptemys ouachitensis*

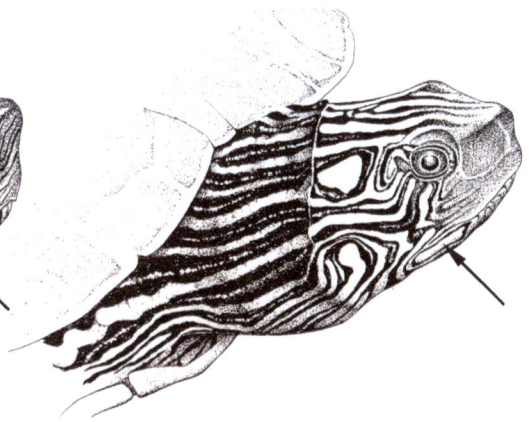

Northern Map Turtle, *Graptemys geographica*

Reptile and Amphibian Conservation and Management

In the past three decades, reptiles and amphibian populations have declined world-wide. Habitat loss may be the single biggest cause of species declines but other reported factors include disease (Chytridiomycosis), climate change, pollution and chemical contaminants, ozone depletion, ultraviolet radiation, introduced predators, and trematodes.

Without question, protecting remaining forestlands from development is an important step toward safeguarding residual reptile and amphibian populations. But what about grasslands? Restricting growth of trees in these ecosystems can actually have positive benefits to herpetofauna as well. While highly manicured grasslands such as mowed lawns provide little habitat for reptiles and amphibians, grasslands mowed only once a year can be exceptional environments for a number of species, especially snakes. Why? Their food sources (primarily small rodents and invertebrates) thrive in these "old field" conditions and decline or disappear in highly domesticated ones. Unkempt fields are also magnets for a whole host of other species including butterflies, moths, bats, and birds. This is because old fields have much richer plant communities. So if you want a show, let it grow!

In addition to leaving wild spaces wild, placing old roofing tin or boards along woodland edges will attract snakes and lizards, not to mention a whole host of other fascinating creatures. Boards placed in the woods will attract salamanders. Flipping tin, logs, and rocks has become a pastime for our kids and more recently, our grand-kids. Watching children mesmerized by bugs, spiders, earthworms, lizards, and salamanders is utterly enjoyable and a kick-starter to that sense of wonder we all had as kids. It's like a treasure hunt and every object turned hides a different surprise. Any overturned object should always be returned to its original place to protect the micro -climate of the site.

Ponds

People often ask me, "what's the single best thing I can do for wildlife"? My answer is always unequivocally water. Besides allowing wild places on your property to grow feral, building a small pond or two will bring in more wildlife than any other single management practice. Ponds should be small around 10 to 15 feet in diameter and can be either roundish or oblong in shape and no more than a few feet deep. Even if the pond dries up in mid to late summer (referred to as a vernal pond) salamander, frog, and invertebrate larvae have already metamorphosed. **Keep Fish Out Of These Small Ponds**! Fish will do poorly in such a diminutive environment and more importantly, eat the larvae of frogs, salamanders, and dragonflies.

Believe it or not, one of the best ways to control mosquito populations is to build a pond. This may sound counterintuitive but here is the uncanny twist. Mosquitoes (food) lay their eggs (food) in the ponds which hatch into free swimming larva (food). This is a plus for two other groups of organisms attracted to water to complete their reproductive life stages. The first group includes the dragonflies and damselflies, which are often referred to as mosquito-hawks. Adult dragonflies and dam-

197

selflies are predacious on a number of small insects including adult mosquitoes. The second, and perhaps more important group in terms of their ability to obliterate mosquito populations are salamanders, or more precisely their larva. Adult mole salamanders (Spotted, Jefferson, Tiger, and Marbled) come to fishless ponds to lay their eggs in large numbers. When the salamander larvae hatch, they have only one thing on their mind; eat mosquito larvae and other small invertebrates. So adult mosquitoes are consumed by dragonflies, and mosquito larvae are eaten by the larvae of salamanders. Besides the pure joy of watching life cycles play out in your pond, you get one of the nature's best biological mosquito controls, without the use of anthropogenic pesticides! How cool is that?

The construction of a small pond can be accomplished in a number of ways. Choose a site that has a high clay content. A small dozer (350 to 450) can dig and finish a pond in around two hours. An excavator is also a good choice and will do a satisfactory job with perhaps less impact to the overall site. Lastly, small ponds can be dug by hand or you can purchase one of those small plastic water ponds. Remember ponds don't need to be large to be effective breeding habitat for dragonflies and amphibians. "A Guide To Creating Vernal Ponds" by Tom Biebighauser is a great resource for information regarding pond construction techniques.

A newly dug pond, RRG

Same pond one year later

A small pond constructed with a 350 bulldozer, Gritter Ridge, Powell County, Kentucky

GLOSSARY

AMPLEXUS, AMPLEXING: the mating position in frogs and toads; the male clasps the female about the back.

ANAL SCALE (OR PLATE): the scale of a snake just in front of and covering the cloaca; can be a single scale or paired scales.

ANTERIOR: front of an animal.

ANURAN: a tailless amphibian in the order of *Anura*; a frog or toad.

BARBELS: a whisker-like organ near the mouth of turtles.

CARAPACE: the upper shell of a turtle.

CLOACA: a single opening that serves as the only orifice that connects the digestive, reproductive and urinary tracts present in reptiles, amphibians, birds, and most fish.

CONGRESS: a group of salamanders.

COSTAL FOLDS: the spaces between the costal grooves.

COSTAL GROOVES: vertical grooves on the flanks of salamanders.

CAUDAL AUTONOMY: the ability to drop a tail as in some lizards.

DORSAL: the upper surface.

DORSOLATERAL FOLD: raised ridges of skin that run down part or all of the length of the back of some frog species like *Lithobates*.

ENDEMIC: indigenous or confined to a certain region.

FOSSORIAL: adapted to digging and life underground like mole salamanders.

GRAVID: pregnant; carrying eggs or young.

HERPETOFAUNA: the reptiles and amphibians of a region, habitat or geological period.

NARES: the nostrils.

NASOLABIAL GROOVE: vertical slit between the nostril and the lip, line with glands that aid in chemoreception.

OPISTHOGLYPHOUS: back-fanged.

PARATOID GLANDS: a pair of wart-like glands on the shoulder, neck, or back of the eye in toads.

PLASTRON: the lower shell of a turtle.

POSTERIOR: the rear or back surface.

SPERMATOPHORE: a protein capsule containing a mass of spermatozoa exchanged during mating in salamanders.

SPIRACLE: a tube-like opening on the left side in most kinds of tadpoles where respiratory water exits.

TYMPANUM: the eardrum.

VENTRAL: the bottom surface.

VERNAL POND: temporary or ephemeral pond or pools of water that provide habitat for specific plants and animals.

BIBLIOGRAPHY

The list below includes references used in this book as well as other pertinent resources should you wish further information.

ALLEN, W. L., R. J. BADDELEY, N. SCOTT-SAMUEL, I. C. CUTHILL. 2013. The evolution and function of pattern diversity in snakes. Behavioral Ecology 24(5):1237-1250.

ARNOLD, S. J. 1976. Sexual behavior, sexual interference, and sexual defense in the salamanders, *Ambystoma maculatum, Ambystoma tigrinum*, and *Plethodon jordani*. Zeitschrift für Tierpsychologie 42:247-300.

BEHLER, J. L, & F. W. KING. 1979. The Audubon Society field guide to North American reptiles and amphibians. Alfred E. Knopf. New York, NY. 719 pp.

CAMPBELL, J. J. N., D. T. TOWLES, J. R. MACGREGOR, R. R. CICERELLO, B. PALMER-BALL, JR., M. E. MEDLEY, S. OLSON. 1989. Cooperative inventory of endangered, threatened, sensitive and rare species, Daniel Boone National Forest, Stanton Ranger District. Cooperators: USDA Forest Service, The Nature Conservancy, Kentucky State Nature Preserves Commission, and Kentucky Department of Fish and Wildlife Resources. Report submitted February 1989 to the Daniel Boone National Forest. Winchester, KY. 316 p.

CLARK, R.W., M.N. MARCHAND, B.J. CLIFFORD, R. STECHERT, AND S. STEPHENS. 2010. Decline of an isolated timber rattlesnake (Crotalus horridus) population: Interactions between climate change, disease, and loss of genetic diversity. Biological Conservation 144:886-891.

CONANT, R. & J. T. COLLINS. 1998. A field guide to reptiles and amphibians, eastern and central North America. Houghton Mifflin Company, New York, NY. Peterson Field Guide Series. 616 pp.

HUTTON, C. E. 2017. The diet of the Cumberland Plateau Salamander (Plethodon kentucki) in an old growth forest of southeastern Kentucky. American Midland Naturalist (in press).

KAHN, C. M. 2010. Ed. Merck Veterinary Manual, Tenth edition. 2945 pp.

LILLYWHITE, H. 2015. How snakes work: structure, function and behavior of the world's snakes. Oxford University Press. 256 pp.

MEERBURG, B. G., G. R. SINGLETON, A. KIJLSTRA. 2009. Rodent-borne diseases and their risk for public health. Critical Review in Microbiology 35(3):221-270.

PETRANKA, J. W. 1998. Salamanders of the United States and Canada. Washington, D. C., USA: Smithsonian Institution Press.

RAJEEV, S., D.A. SUTTON, B.L. WICKES, D.L. MILLER, D. GIRI, M. VANMETER, E.H. THOMPSON, M.G. RINALDI, A.M. ROMANELLI, J.F. CANO, AND J. GUARRO. 2009. Isolation and characterization of a new fungal species, Chrysosporium ophiodiicola, from a mycotic granuloma of a black rat snake *(Elaphe obsoleta obsoleta)*. Journal of Clinical Microbiology 47:1264-1268.

READING, C. J., L. M. LUISELLI, G. C. AKANI, X. BONNET, G. AMORI, J.M. BALLOUARD, E.FILLIPI, G. NAULLEAU, D. PEARSON, L. RUGIERO. 2010. Are snake populations in decline? Biology Letter 6:777–780 doi:10.1098/rsbl.2010.0373 Published online 9 June 2010.

STAFFORD, P. J. & J. R. MEYER. 2000 A guide to the reptiles and amphibians of Belize. The Natural History Museum, London. 356 pp.

STOREY K.B & STOREY J.M. 1984. Biochemical adaption for freezing tolerance in the wood frog, *Rana sylvatica*. Journal of Comparative Physiology B. 155: 29–36.

Reptile and Amphibian Checklist 2021

Anurans (Frogs & Toads) (14 species confirmed, 1 species not yet confirmed)
- ☐ American Bullfrog *Lithobates catesbeianus* (Shaw, 1802)
- ☐ American Toad *Anaxyrus americanus* (Holbrook, 1836)
- ☐ Blanchard's Cricket Frog *Acris blanchardi* Harper, 1947
- ☐ Cope's Gray Treefrog *Hyla chrysoscelis* Cope, 1880
- ☐ **Eastern Narrow-mouthed Toad *Gastrophryne carolinensis*** (Holbrook, 1836) **(IN)**
- ☐ Eastern Spadefoot *Scaphiopus holbrookii* (Harlan, 1835)
- ☐ Fowler's Toad *Anaxyrus fowleri* (Hinckley, 1882)
- ☐ Green Frog *Lithobates clamitans* (Latreille, 1801)
- ☐ Mountain Chorus Frog *Pseudacris brachypona* (Cope, 1889)
- ☐ Northern Leopard Frog *Lithobates pipiens* (Schreber, 1782)
- ☐ Pickerel Frog *Lithobates palustris* (LeConte, 1825)
- ☐ Southern Leopard Frog *Lithobates sphenocephalus* (Cope, 1886)
- ☐ Spring Peeper *Pseudacris crucifer* (Wied-Neuwied, 1883)
- ☐ **Upland Chorus Frog *Pseudacris feriarum*** (Baird, 1854) **(NYC)**
- ☐ Wood Frog *Lithobates sylvaticus* (LeConte, 1825)

Lizards (5 species confirmed)
- ☐ Broad-headed Skink *Plestiodon laticeps* (Schneider, 1801)
- ☐ Coal Skink *Plestiodon anthracinus* (Baird, 1850)
- ☐ Common Five-lined Skink *Plestiodon fasciatus* (Linnaeus, 1758)
- ☐ Eastern Fence Lizard *Sceloporus undulatus* (Bosc and Daudin in Sonnini and Latreille, 1801)
- ☐ Little Brown Skink *Scincella lateralis* (Say in James, 1822)

Salamanders (22 species confirmed, 1 species not yet confirmed)
- ☐ Allegheny Mountain Dusky Salamander *Desmognathus ochrophaeus* Cope, 1859
- ☐ Black Mountain Salamander *Desmognathus welteri* Barbour, 1950
- ☐ Cave Salamander *Eurycea lucifuga* Rafinesque, 1822
- ☐ Cumberland Plateau Salamander *Plethodon kentucki* Mittleman, 1951
- ☐ Eastern Newt *Notophthalmus viridescens* (Rafinesque, 1820)
- ☐ Four-toed Salamander *Hemidactylium scutatum* (Temminck & Schlegel in Von Siebold, 1838)
- ☐ Green Salamander *Aneides aeneus* (Cope & Packard, 1881)
- ☐ Eastern Hellbender *Cryptobranchus alleganiensis* (Daudin, 1803)
- ☐ Jefferson Salamander *Ambystoma jeffersonianum* (Green, 1827)
- ☐ Long-tailed Salamander *Eurycea longicauda* (Green, 1818)
- ☐ Marbled Salamander *Ambystoma opacum* (Gravenhorst, 1807)
- ☐ Midland Mud Salamander *Pseudotriton montanus diastictus* Bishop, 1941
- ☐ Mudpuppy *Necturus maculosus* (Rafinesque, 1818)
- ☐ Northern Dusky Salamander *Desmognathus fuscus* (Rafinesque, 1820)
- ☐ Northern Slimy Salamander *Plethodon glutinosus* (Green, 1818)
- ☐ **Northern Zigzag Salamander *Plethodon dorsalis*** Cope, 1886 **(NYC)**
- ☐ Red Salamander *Pseudotriton ruber* (Latreille, 1801)
- ☐ Seal Salamander *Desmognathus monticola* Dunn, 1916
- ☐ Southern Ravine Salamander *Plethodon richmondi* Netting & Mittleman, 1938

- ☐ Southern Two-lined Salamander *Eurycea cirrigera* (Green, 1830)
- ☐ Kentucky Spring Salamander *Gyrinophilus porphyriticus duryi* (Green, 1827)
- ☐ Spotted Salamander *Ambystoma maculatum* (Shaw, 1802)
- ☐ Streamside Salamander *Ambystoma barbouri* Kraus & Petranka, 1989

Snakes (18 species confirmed, 1 species not yet confirmed)

- ☐ Eastern Black Kingsnake *Lampropeltis nigra* (Yarrow, 1882)
- ☐ Common Gartersnake *Thamnophis sirtalis* (Linnaeus, 1758)
- ☐ Common Watersnake *Nerodia sipedon* (Linnaeus, 1758)
- ☐ Common Wormsnake *Carphophis amoenus* ((Say, 1825)
- ☐ Dekay's Brownsnake *Storeria dekayi* (Holbrook, 1836)
- ☐ Eastern Copperhead *Agkistrodon contortrix* (Linnaeus, 1766)
- ☐ Eastern Hog-nosed Snake *Heterodon platyrhinos* Latreille, 1801
- ☐ Eastern Milksnake *Lampropeltis triangulum* (Lacépède, 1789)
- ☐ Gray Ratsnake *Pantherophis spiloides* (Duméril, Bibron & Duméril, 1854)
- ☐ North American Racer *Coluber constrictor* Linnaeus, 1758
- ☐ Queensnake *Regina septemvittata* (Say, 1825)
- ☐ Red-bellied Snake *Storeria occipitomaculata* (Storer, 1839)
- ☐ Red Cornsnake *Pantherophis guttatus* (Linnaeus, 1766)
- ☐ Ring-necked Snake *Diadophis punctatus* (Linnaeus, 1766)
- ☐ Rough Greensnake *Opheodrys aestivus* (Linnaeus, 1766)
- ☐ **Scarlet Kingsnake *Lampropeltis elapsoides* (Holbrook, 1838) (NYC)**
- ☐ Scarletsnake *Cemophora coccinea* (Blumenbach, 1788)
- ☐ Smooth Earthsnake *Virginia valeriae* Baird & Girard, 1853
- ☐ Timber Rattlesnake *Crotalus horridus* Linnaeus, 1758

Turtles (7 species confirmed, 1 species not yet confirmed)

- ☐ Eastern Box Turtle *Terrapene carolina* (Linnaeus, 1758)
- ☐ Eastern Musk Turtle *Sternotherus odoratus* (Latreille, 1802)
- ☐ Eastern Spiny Softshell *Apalone spinifera* (LeSueur, 1827)
- ☐ Northern Map Turtle *Graptemys geographica* (LeSueur, 1817)
- ☐ **Ouachita Map Turtle *Graptemys ouachitensis* Cagle, 1953 (NYC)**
- ☐ Painted Turtle *Chrysemys picta* (Schneider, 1783)
- ☐ Pond Slider *Trachemys scripta* (Thunberg in Schoepff, 1792)
- ☐ Snapping Turtle *Chelydra serpentina* (Schweigger, 1812)

Index of Common Names

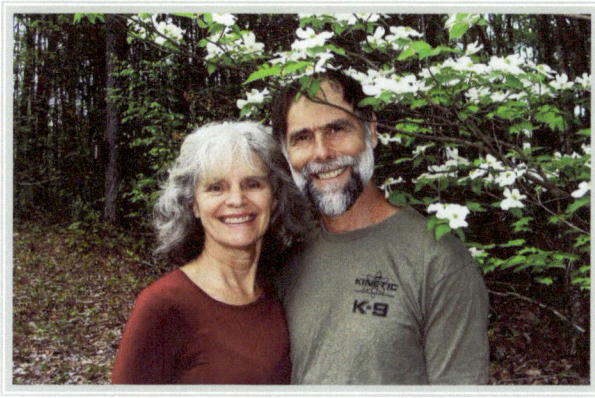

ABOUT THE AUTHORS

Dan Dourson is a biologist/naturalist/illustrator who has spent most of his adult life dedicated to the preservation, conservation, and understanding of the planet's more obscure animals. For nearly twenty years, Dan worked with the US Forest Service, where he was a wildlife biologist specializing in nongame management in Red River Gorge. During his time with the Forest Service, he facilitated the creation of ridgetop ponds for the purpose of amphibian breeding. Dan was part of a collaborative survey for reptiles and amphibians at Wildlife Management Areas (WMA) across the state of Kentucky with state herpetologist, John MacGregor, and biologist, Mark Gumbert. Dan has also conducted herp surveys in South Dakota, Florida and Belize.

In addition, Dan has spent more than 20 years studying land snails in the Eastern United States, Belize, Guatemala, Costa Rica, Panama, and in the Amazon Jungle of northwestern Peru. Dan was one of two lead investigators on a 2016 National Geographic Expedition into the Maya Mountains of Belize, studying a bottom up relationship between land snails and harpy eagles. Dan has described 9 new land snail species from the US and 18 new species from Belize, Central America.

Dan is the author of eight Natural History books including *Wild Yet Tasty*, *Biodiversity of the Maya Mountains, Belize, Central America*, *Wild Flowers and Ferns of Red River Gorge* and four field guides to the land snails of Kentucky, the Great Smoky Mountains National Park and Southern Appalachians, West Virginia and Belize, Central America. He has illustrated nature books and *Wildflowers and Ferns of Kentucky, How Snakes Work,* and multiple environmental posters used in schools around Kentucky.

Dan and Judy managed a Biological Field Station called BFREE (Belize Foundation for Research and Environmental Education) for 7 years in the wild jungles of Central America. Judy Dourson is a retired educator who has served as Dan's field technician, research assistant, and editor for twenty-two years, as well as being his favorite wife! Their family includes Austin (Samantha), Angela (Colby), and Tyler (Jordan) as well as five grandchildren: Zach, Tessa, Callie, Jude, and Kyle.

Dan and Judy remain committed to conservation work protecting the Earth's most amazing and underappreciated organisms. Their passion for the natural world is clearly reflected through their writing and simple lifestyle.